WILL YOU MURDER MY HUSBAND?

CATHERINE NEVIN AND THE IRA

GERARD DOHERTY

ACKNOWLEDGEMENTS

Thanks to:

Jackie, Philip, Clive, Shannon and new arrival Sinéad for your love and support
my parents Patrick and Toni; my brothers Thomas and Stephen and my sister Liz for your guidance and patience
my grandfather Anthony Jennings and my aunts and uncles for instilling in me the confidence needed to write this book
the Gardaí and the Nevin family for their contribution
the staff at Marino Books, particularly Jo and Seán, for the break
the lads of 79 for your encouragement
Special thanks to the principal contributors, named and unnamed, particularly 'The Duke' and J. J.
And in memory of Hilda Jennings, William, Winifred and John Doherty, Brian (Bernie-John) Sheerin and Tom Nevin

Contents

Introduction

The phenomenon that is Catherine Nevin has already spawned two books from two fine journalists. What scope is there then for a third book on the subject?

There is scope for such a book because the Catherine Nevin story has been painted on a giant canvas, of which only parts are visible. Much has been written about Nevin herself, and some have even tried to get a handle on her psyche, but at the time of writing there is no unanimity on exactly what her motivation was. We know she was money-hungry and greedy but it seems that she took just as much satisfaction from manipulating those close to her, and it is in her relationships with other people that she reveals herself. The focus of this book, then, is Catherine Nevin, but the emphasis is slightly different.

Her life before the court case and imprisonment was one of intrigue, manipulation, decadence and ultimately murder, and the examination of that life in microscopic detail has opened a proverbial can of worms. Many lives have been touched by her actions and some have been ruined by them; other people still have questions to answer.

One of the many unique aspects of the Nevin trial is the IRA's involvement in it. Never before had republicans assisted in a case brought by the state, nor had they ever sanctioned one of their members to give evidence. In fact, republicans had not even recognised the jurisdiction of the courts until recently. The fact that, in the end, Catherine Nevin's fate would rest on the evidence of two republicans and a con-man only served to raise the public and media interest in her case to unprecedented levels.

How did the IRA members come to be there and what exactly was their relationship with Catherine Nevin? Why did they agree to testify at her trial? The Nevin case raised many questions about the accused's republican connections, and few were answered properly. The aim of this book is to answer those questions and more.

The difficulty in introducing other unnamed republicans, together with the ferocity of Senior Counsel Patrick McEntee's cross-examination, meant that a great deal was left undiscovered. Many of the lines of enquiry pursued by the defence to unsettle the principal witnesses were quickly blocked or diverted by Gerry Heapes and John Jones, but this author, who has had exclusive access to these two republicans, has been afforded the opportunity to dig further.

Just like the defence team, I have come up against similar obstacles, where the men in question have reached a point beyond which they will not go. From there I have had to make the journey alone – and not exactly with their blessing either. It is safe to say that they are unhappy with some of the steps I have taken. They have agreed, however, that as the author of the book I am responsible for what I have written.

I did not attend the court proceedings but followed the trial with interest and paid careful attention to everything that was written or said about the case. My association with the three principal witnesses as a group began when the case started and I had been asked to act as a sort of media adviser. Not that my advice was ever listened to, however.

Ironically, when the two men were approached by journalists Liz Walsh of *Magill* magazine and Niamh O'Connor of *Ireland on Sunday* to contribute to their respective books, I advised them to go ahead, saying that both Walsh and O'Connor were respectable journalists with excellent track records, but the two men declined to cooperate with either journalist.

What struck me about Heapes, Jones and McClean was that they felt rather misrepresented in the case and that each of them had more to say about it. What started off as a conversation became an interview, and what was once the outline for a newspaper article evolved into this book.

And then I stepped back from the project. I have worked on and off for the last few years as a doorman and during that time have worked with one of the witnesses and contributors, Gerry Heapes. Like a juror who lets it be known that he knows one of the witnesses, I had to accept that my objectivity and perhaps my integrity as a journalist was compromised by this relationship and I decided to shelve the idea of writing a book on the Nevin case.

It soon became clear, however, that If I did not tell the story, no one would, and the background to the most talked-about case in Irish legal history would never be heard. As I dug further into the story, it became clear that the story of the third republican, Patrick Russell, aka John Ferguson, was the most interesting and most shocking of the three. Indeed, in his testimony, Russell spoke of Catherine Nevin in glowing terms.

While researching Russell, I came across so much material that it would have filled a book on its own, but a great deal of this material has little or no relevance to Russell's relationship with Catherine Nevin. Instead I have offered an abridged version which gives the reader some idea of Russell's character.

In writing this book, I have been constrained by Ireland's draconian libel laws but I have left the door open in some cases for others who are better-resourced to take the story further. I have tried to apply the highest journalistic standards to the process of information-gathering and to the treatment of that information, but my dealings with republicans have often made these aspirations difficult to adhere to.

Very often, I was in a position where the only person I could contact to corroborate what I had just been told was Catherine Nevin and, not surprisingly, she refused to comment. In some cases, information gathered was corroborated by other republicans who wished to remain nameless; the fact that they wanted to remain anonymous does not necessarily mean that they were not telling the truth.

Willie McClean, although not a republican, was of paramount importance to the prosecution case. Therefore, despite the fact that his story might seem to fall outside the remit of this book, I have included his contributions because I consider them necessary to help the reader understand Catherine Nevin and what motivated her.

To my mind, aside from her complicity in the murder of her husband, perhaps the worst act Catherine Nevin has perpetrated – and there are many – was to tarnish the reputation of a good man, Tom Nevin. His family knew what type of person he was, and so too did the staff of Jack White's Inn, and they will not be swayed in their view of him. Nonetheless, the claims made by Catherine Nevin that her husband had an IRA background, though largely dismissed, raised some questions that could not be answered in court. In this book, I will endeavour to answer those questions and restore Tom Nevin's good name.

Gerard Doherty
October 2000

1

Dramatis Personae

John Jones
Born on 12 November 1944, John Jones was a latecomer
to the republican cause. His early years were spent,
uneventfully, in Donnycarney, north-east Dublin, but a
growing awareness of politics and the drive for civil
rights in the 1960s ignited a rebellious streak in him.
A job as a salesman with a TV-repair outlet in Santry
marked the end of his childhood, while the fondness
for communism and the writings of Karl Marx that he
developed in his early twenties heralded the beginning
of a subversive lifestyle. He was an avid reader from
an early stage and he digested whatever texts on
communism he could get his hands on, including
Marx's *Das Kapital* and *The Communist Manifesto.*

Jones received his primary education in St Kieran's
in Donnycarney and his secondary education at St
Joseph's in Fairview – both schools on Dublin's north-
side. His communist leanings alarmed the authorities
and he was sent on scholarship to the Jesuit Catholic
Workers – an early effort by the Catholic Church to
counter the threat of communism. But Jones, who was
already familar with what was taught there, left because
he could not reconcile the two philosophies. He
repudiated Catholicism's kowtowing to capitalism and

became a regular visitor to the left-wing bookshop that at the time was situated beside Tara Street Fire Station. In the early 1960s, proving both his sincerity and his nerve, he jumped on to a car that contained Edward Kennedy, instructing him to tell his brother to get the troops out of Vietnam.

At that stage he came under the influence of the writings of James Connolly, writings that combined socialism and republicanism. He bought *The United Irishman* on a regular basis, and described himself as an 'agrarian anti-capitalist', but Connolly's insistence that the war with the colonial oppressor had to be won before a just system could be established resonated with him. It became inevitable that he should join the republican movement.

He remained, however, an active socialist. He founded SCARF (Strike Committee for Aid and Relief) during the Smurfit strike in the late 1970s. Members of SCARF spread word of the plight of striking workers and funded unofficial strikes, much to the displeasure of the established trade union movement. He had been a member of the ITGWU (Irish Transport and General Workers' Union) but left it to join Matt Merrigan's ATGWU (Amalgamated Transport and General Workers' Union).

By 1969 he had gravitated towards the republican movement, which was just about to split into the Official and Provisional factions. With his communist leanings he might have been expected to side with the Officials but the situation forced a snap decision and he decided to join the Provisionals. In the same year he participated in several civil rights marchs, in both the North and the South, and he was horrified at the attacks on the marchers. In 1971 he was arrested by the RUC in Derry in the company of the brother of the then editor of *An Phoblacht*. The two men were detained for about five hours.

The sight of the Bogside under siege in pre-Bloody Sunday Derry left an indelible mark on Jones: he was incensed that people in one part of the island could allow people on another part of it to be driven out of their homes, beaten and killed. He resolved there and then to inform people about what was going on in the North.

By the beginning of the 1970s, he was a fully fledged member of the James Connolly Cumann of Sinn Féin in Rathmines. He was also heavily involved in Cabhair Uladh, an organisation set up by republicans to raise funds for families displaced by the violence in the North. It was an interesting concept, facilitated by the Wolfe Tone Society, which brought together under one umbrella members of the official and provisional factions of the republican movement and members of the civil rights movement.

In the early 1970s, a young man called Dessie Ellis began an apprenticeship as a trainee technician in Kilroy's, and he and Jones soon became good friends. Jones was now married and living in Artane, and in 1978 he and Ellis went into business together, first working out of Ellis's garage, and then setting up Channel Vision, a TV hire and repair shop at 2A Church Street in Finglas.

'We saw an opening,' Jones recalls. 'The people we worked for would only repair TVs if they were under warranty, and lots of good business was turned away. We aimed at that customer base. There were many people who couldn't afford to buy a TV, and for them rental was the only option. We were able to service their needs too.'

He and Ellis were, he reckons, placed under surveillance pretty much from the day they opened, but this surveillance was covert, and was conducted by a division of the Special Branch specialising in surveillance. Their brief was surveillance only: they neither openly engaged their targets, nor did they ever identify themselves. 'They could be anybody, a man or woman, young or old, on foot, in a car or on a motorcycle,' says Jones.

Special Branch proper did not enter the fray until Dessie Ellis was arrested in 1981; after that point, Jones's life would never be the same again. On the morning of the raid, about thirty-five or forty friends and associates of his were raided too.

Everything and everyone who went in or out of Channel Vision was watched; some were questioned, others arrested. One incident in particular makes clear the level of interest shown in the workings of the shop. 'I can remember that I had been sent a box of transistor radios in need of repair from Donegal,' Jones recalls, 'and I know for a fact that the sender was a unionist from the east of the county. I sorted out the problems, put the transistor radios back into the box, having repaired them, and arranged to have the parcel taken to Donegal on the CIÉ bus. When the package arrived, so did the gardaí, armed and unarmed, the army, helicopters and all to the gentleman's house. The poor man didn't know what was happening. Needless to say, all they found was a box of transistors.'

Ellis's arrest also coincided with the opening of a Sinn Féin advice centre in the building that housed the TV-repair shop. Special Branch then started to harass customers and raid their homes; the effect of this on the shop's business was catastrophic.

Jones remembers one particular customer from Blanchardstown. 'This guy had come in to rent a television,' he says, 'and things weren't quite ready for him, so I agreed to deliver the TV out to his house whenever it was ready. When I went out to deliver it, the Branch followed me all the way. The same guy arrived back into the shop a few days later with the TV, looking a little flustered. "John," he said, "I'm sorry, but I have to give this back. I didn't realise that a raid by Special Branch was part of the contract." It seems that Special Branch had raided his house, dragged him in and asked him whether he stored gear for me.'

By the time Catherine Nevin entered the fray, the business was collapsing, but it was the start of the 1990s before the shop – and with it the Sinn Féin advice centre – closed. Another business in Balbriggan, where Jones was then living, also bit the dust. 'I had to reinvent myself,' he says. It seems the level of his republican involvement was scaled down, and by the time Tom Nevin was murdered he was running a shuttle-bus service out of the airport and attending night school. So what was – or is – the nature of Jones's republican involvement?

First of all, he has never been convicted of member-ship of the IRA. He freely admits that he was chairman of the Jack McCabe Cumann of Sinn Féin, and it seems he took that responsibility very seriously. Nonetheless, Jones is a talented organiser, an articulate speaker and an excellent strategist, and it seems unlikely that the IRA would let these talents go to waste.

The strongest suggestion that Jones was involved with the IRA came in 1991, when he entered the Irish public's consciousness for the first time. At the Old Bailey in London, Dessie Ellis told the court that Jones was his link to the IRA and Ellis was subsequently acquitted on a charge of conspiracy to commit explosions. In the Nevin trial, Jones told the jury that not alone did he not know anyone in the IRA, he wouldn't even know how to go about contacting the organisation.

Jones has one criminal conviction. On 18 November 1988 he pleaded guilty at Dublin Circuit Court to receiving a stolen car. One day he was leaving the Sinn Féin headquarters in Parnell Square for his parking space in Granby Row when he sensed that he was being followed. He was pulled in by the Special Branch on the north side of the square and a chance remark by one of the gardaí that his car must have been off the road for years set alarm bells ringing. When he checked, he realised that nothing tallied and that the car must have been stolen. He parked the car in the garage at his house and there it remained for about a year, untouched. When Jones did decide to move it, his timing could not have been worse. The Special Branch were watching his house to estabish if he was habouring a prison escaper when Jones drove the car out in full view. After a quick background check, Jones was arrested. He claimed that he had bought the car after following up an advertisement in the newspaper. He received a three-year suspended sentence and was ordered to pay £3,000 to the relevant insurance company and £500 to the owner of the car.

Ironically, the barrister he chose to defend him that day was none other than Patrick McEntee, the Senior Counsel who would defend Nevin at her trial. Jones had enlisted his help primarily because he was one of the best-regarded defence lawyers in the state, and also because Jones was convinced that Special Branch would throw the book at him over the car crime.

Jones is, for the most part, a quiet and unassuming character but he is also a man of deeply held convictions and is not afraid to articulate these views, should the occasion warrant it. Were it not for his new-found notoriety as one of the star witnesses in the trial of Catherine Nevin, there is no doubt that he would have disappeared from view. That kind of life would have suited him perfectly.

Willie McClean

Following Partition in 1920, crossing the border became a livelihood for some of the inhabitants of the border counties. This was the case with Willie McClean's father, for example. When Willie was born, on 13 June 1951, his father was already well established as a cattle-dealer and smuggler.

But then, smuggling was a way of life for many of the residents of Ballinode, County Monaghan, five miles from the county town and three from the border. Cattle, pigs and spirits were the currency of this trade, at least in the early years, when the price difference was huge and the smuggling runs worthwhile.

Willie left school to pursue a career in smuggling full-time, and from the outset he could see that his family's religion, far from being a hindrance, was a godsend when dealing with loyalists north of the border. Ballinode is deep in republican heartland, and Willie knew most of local movers and shakers. It seems, at least in the early years, that he enjoyed the best of both worlds.

Smugglers always ran the risk of arrest or imprisonment, however, and it seems that, by the start of the Troubles in 1969, when the smuggling fraternity was coming under increased pressure, McClean had decided to diversify. He became involved in 'kiting' – a Dublin slang term for the practice of buying goods using cheques drawn on an empty account.

McClean found himself in Clogher Magistrates Court on 26 July 1973 charged with theft by deception – or fraud. He had used a cheque to purchase a Land Rover that he clearly hadn't the money for. He was sentenced to three months in jail, which he appealed, but the charge was upheld in Omagh Magistrates Court. Three months later he was up on a similar charge and received a two-year sentence. A crate of apples that he had kited landed him in court again, this time in a civil case. As before, he was found guilty. With the sentence hanging over his head, crossing the border became a tension-filled experience and Willie began to feel it was time to move on. First, though, he was involved in an incident that almost got him killed.

Dragged by a group of masked men from the Hillgrove Hotel in Monaghan town in March 1974, he was given what amounted to a punishment beating and was lucky to escape with just a few broken ribs. The attack bore all the hallmarks of the IRA but McClean will neither confirm nor deny that it was carried out by IRA members. Moreover, he refuses point-blank to discuss why it happened in the first place. The upshot was that, within a month or two, he had moved permanently to Harold's Cross in Dublin.

McClean began work for a waste-disposal firm but soon went out on his own, selling the business in 1980. An underworld source has revealed that he wasted no time getting to know the locals, particularly one Martin Cahill, aka the General, but when I put this to Willie he claimed that he had been friendly with a few of the General's associates but didn't know the man himself.

Either way, he prospered, and after a brief flirtation with the oil business, he returned to the waste disposal industry, before selling off his business again at the start of the 1990s as a going concern.

He claims that he is now semi-retired, but it is rumoured that he has a financial interest in the piano business next door to his house. With the exception of a brief period living in Kingswood Heights in Tallaght, he has spent most of the years since he arrived from Monaghan in Harold's Cross.

Now in his fiftieth year, McClean retains his strong Monaghan accent and has maintained his links with his birthplace. The subject of some unpleasant comments about his appearence in recent months, he nevertheless professes to having had his fair share of women over the years. There is no denying that he is a colourful character.

Gerry Heapes

Despite their best attempts to steer the civil rights movement in Northern Ireland towards a republican agenda, the IRA, before it split in 1969, had failed to gather much additional support. Then, when the Prime Minister of Northern Ireland, Captain Terence O'Neill, began to introduce some basic human rights for Catholics, the attitude of most was to let him go about his business and repair the yawning divide that was emerging in his own party, the Ulster Unionist Party.

On New Year's Day 1969, however, the Queen's University-based People's Democracy organised a civil rights march from Belfast to Derry, much to the chagrin of the unionist population – and, bizzarely, the Dublin leadership of the IRA. The route was peppered with incidents but the most serious occurred a few miles outside the village of Claudy at Burntollet Bridge, when the marchers were ambushed by a loyalist mob who had been awaiting their arrival. The marchers were first showered with bricks, bottles and stones and then attacked with iron bars and cudgels. The RUC watched the proceedings but made no arrests.

It was discovered later that at least a hundred of the ambush party were off-duty members of the 'B' Specials, the auxiliary force of the RUC, which had been created from the ranks of the Ulster Volunteer Force. This attack, and many similar ones, were being followed by many people south of the border, who were incensed at the behaviour of the RUC. Some went straight out and joined the IRA. The events would provide the touch-paper for the Troubles and would signal the start of the republican career of Gerry Heapes.

Heapes had spent his formative years living on the North Strand in Dublin and in England before his family moved to Finglas in 1960 or 1961. He left school at fourteen and went to work for Burmah Oil, which was based on the quays.

In 1967, he got a job as a porter in the Rotunda Hospital, working under his father, who was head porter there at the time. He left Dublin briefly in 1971 to work for Briggs and Masco, a felting company, before becoming head porter in the Jervis Street Hospital a year later. He would keep that position until his arrest and imprisonment in 1977.

The most significant incident in Heapes's years as a porter was undoubtedly the 1974 bombings, where four bombs prepared by loyalists – allegedly assisted by British intelligence forces – exploded in Dublin and Monaghan, killing thirty people in what was the worst single incident in the Troubles.

Jervis Street Hospital received the brunt of the dead and injured, and as head porter it was Heapes's responsibility to coordinate the removal of the bodies from the ambulance. 'It was like hell on earth,' he recalls. 'At one stage I had a box of feet and hands and other body parts and I had to match them with the victims. We took in one person who had almost been cut in two by a traffic sign, and the sign was still lodged in his stomach. We had to pull it out.'

Some of the victims were from Heapes's native Finglas, and this only made the job harder. Many of the porters worked three days straight, and it was only at the end of this time that they grasped the enormity of what had happened. Counselling for staff in the hospital was unheard of in the early 1970s, and the men were left to deal with what they had just witnessed on their own.

Heapes had been drawn to the republican movement in the late 1960s, but the new decade had begun before he became active in it. He joined an active-service unit whose responsibility it was to procure funds to buy arms for the movement: this meant armed robberies.

With no hard evidence of his complicity in earlier robberies, one can only assume that, to begin with, the unit was successful wherever it robbed. This run of luck ended in mid-October 1977, however, when Heapes and seven others were arrested when they tried to hold up Leyden's Cash and Carry on the Richmond Road near Croke Park. The cash and carry had been the scene of a successful robbery a few weeks earlier – though whether the earlier robbery had been carried out by the same gang is not clear. Either way, the IRA decided to have a go.

The operation was a disaster from start to finish. To begin with, apart from a couple of pounds in a cash box in the manager's office, there was nothing for them to rob and they were laughed at by the staff. Then one of the drivers ran in to say that the gardaí had the place surrounded. Heapes took this to mean the ordinary gardaí, and he felt confident he would effect an escape with pistols in both hands. When he reached the cordon, he was horrified to discover that the officers surrounding the cash and carry were not gardaí but Special Branch; he was immediately arrested.

Inside the cash and carry, a hostage situation had developed. There were no demands made for money.

Instead, the IRA men wanted to make people aware of the tactics used by the branch of the gardaí who were known unofficially as 'the heavy mob'.

A priest from Dominic Street who was also the chaplain in Jervis Street Hospital was the first to intercede, before the Archbishop himself arrived. While in the office with the IRA men, the Archbishop lit up his pipe – or rather, it was lit for him using some of the money from the cash box. The situation was soon over and the rest of the gang arrested.

Two weeks later the men were brought before the court and, because they did not recognise its jurisdiction, they had no legal representation. The mood among the men was jovial and they decided to draw cards to predict how many years they would get. Heapes drew the two of hearts – but got ten years. He was convicted of several charges: armed robbery, membership of the IRA and possession of firearms, all of which carried sentences of between six and eight years, but in the end the judge decided to have them run concurrently in a ten-year stretch.

With many of the others receiving similar sentences, the men were bound for Portlaoise, which was now the primary holding centre for republicans. The mood was still upbeat. Many of the lads had grown up with Heapes and the camaraderie between them cushioned the blow of the jail terms. They resolved to see their sentences out together.

The IRA approach to incarceration is well known, given that many of the organisation's members have spent years in prison. Inside Portlaoise, as in the Maze Prison in the North, a chain of command was established, with all IRA prisoners answerable to the Officer Commanding. In the prison, there would be drilling and many of the other trappings of an army. When Heapes entered Portlaoise in late 1977, however, no such arrangements existed.

In Portlaoise Prison there was a rift among the republican prisoners between the larger, Provisional element and a smaller group loyal to Dominic McGlinchey. Things soon came to a head. All the republican prisoners were given the option of either following orders by the next Monday or leaving the landing. If they refused to move, they would be forcibly removed. On the Monday about twelve men, including McGlinchey, left the prison landing, leaving the larger body of some forty to fifty republicans loyal to the OC. The IRA adopted a prisoner-of-war attitude: there would be no association with the prison authorities except through official channels – that is, through a designated republican prisoner.

There was a concerted attempt to teach the less-educated, and lectures were given by the more erudite scholars among the IRA's ranks on all sorts of subjects, political and otherwise. Heapes, who had left school at fourteen, derived great benefit from these lessons. There was a heavy emphasis on craft-making, and Heapes was taught woodworking by another prisoner. Craftwork pieces were made inside and sold outside to help prisoners' families. Ironically, Catherine Nevin would buy one such item.

Conditions in the prison were never as bad as in the Maze – especially before and during the hunger strikes – but the inmates hated the authorities and went to great lengths to make their jobs more difficult. Strip-searching was a regular occurrence in the prison, and the IRA prisoners were under orders to put up as much resistance as possible when prison officers tried to strip-search them. Only elderly and infirm republicans were exempt from this order and many of those who resisted were badly injured.

This didn't dampen the IRA members' enthusiasm, however, and Heapes maintains that the camaraderie between them made the time go quickly. He was almost sad to leave when he was told he would be released after eight years. But a wife and five children – one born while he was inside – needed him too and his release would signal the end of his active republican career.

Heapes had lived in Blanchardstown in west Dublin before his incarceration but by the time he was released in 1985 the family had moved to Ballygall Crescent in Finglas. Immediately after his release, he set about finding work, and he was told by old work colleagues that there were two vacancies for porters in Jervis Street Hospital. When he arrived at the hospital, however, he was told he would not even be given an interview. Incensed, he contacted the ITGWU but they could do nothing, and the Archbishop, when contacted, told Heapes that he agreed with the hospital's stance.

He finally got work on the door of the Black Sheep pub in Coolock and remained there for a while. Special Branch had decided to keep a close eye on him and make things difficult for him whenever they could, and when they found out where he was working they made a direct approach to the owner of the pub. There was a series of raids on his house, all calculated to ensure that Heapes did not resume his republican activities.

'I didn't mind the hassle,' Heapes says. 'It was all part of the mind games we played with them. But I did take exception to the way my family were treated.'

Steady work came from a man named Alan Gannon, who at the time was one of the biggest independent security operators in the country. At one stage Gannon was responsible for security at Lansdowne Road, Croke Park, Slane and the Point. He was also one of four men arrested with Heapes and brought to Enniscorthy for questioning prior to the Nevin trial.

Gannon stuck with Heapes and got him work on the door of a club called Samantha's on Leeson Street, but it wasn't long before Heapes was moving on again. This time, the opportunity to work as a doorman for a pub closer to home arose, and for the first and only time – contrary to other reports – he worked the door of the Barry House, or Cappagh House as it was then known. He worked at the Cappagh House for eighteen months before moving next door to the pool hall, which he ran for a further six months. It wasn't long, however, before he was back with Gannon, who proceeded to use him everywhere. Special Branch had eased off Heapes a bit but still demanded to know his whereabouts, working hours and travelling arrangements whenever they saw fit.

When the English fans ran amok at Lansdowne Road in 1994, Heapes again found himself plastered all over the papers, but this time in a case of mistaken identity. Spotting an old man getting beaten at the hands of three English thugs, Heapes implored the gardaí to intercede. When they didn't, he jumped in and took on all three Englishmen, eventually getting all three to the ground, where he kicked them a few times. This was caught on camera, and the picture was run by virtually every newspaper the next day, with Heapes identified as an English thug. *Ireland on Sunday* used the picture as recently as late 1999, when it ran an article on the hooligan element in English football.

Heapes then went to work for a man named Luke O'Reilly, who had a security company which used dogs. The venture didn't last long, and O'Reilly went on to chauffeur none other than Patrick Russell, who was doing quite well for himself. In 1995 Heapes went to work for a man named Brian Capper of On The Spot Security in the Waterfront on Sir John Rogerson's Quay. The venue, which was used in the film *The Commitments,* had become a drugs haven, and it was raided and closed down in the weeks before Capper took over. Heapes is well-known for his distaste for drugs, and it wasn't long before the Waterfront was a drug-free zone. Capper and his company were commended by the local gardaí on several occasions for their part in the war against drugs.

When the club closed in 1998, Capper placed Heapes first in the Black Sheep – at that time known as the Oak Tavern – and then in the Bottom of the Hill pub in Finglas, not far from the house in Ballygall Crescent that Heapes and his family had left when they moved to Harristown Lane in Saint Margaret's in north County Dublin.

After his release from prison, Heapes had joined Sinn Féin, where he met John Jones, Tommy Thompson and, eventually, Catherine Nevin. He left the Cumann after a few months, citing his wish to spend more time with his family as his reason for going.

Heapes is a big man and would have gained a reputation even before he went to prison as someone who could handle himself. His status as an armed robber, albeit one acting for the IRA, would have earned him respect among blaggers, and the fact that he had carried guns and certainly knew how to use them made him a frightening proposition.

Anyone who has approached him, however, would say that he is affable and charming. His friends know him as a practical joker and storyteller without equal and, regardless of how those within the republican movement perceive him, he is probably one of the most respected men in Finglas.

Catherine Nevin would have known a great deal about him before she met him, and it seems that, even though she would approach John Jones, another member of the same *cumann,* to murder Tom Nevin she obviously believed that both men represented different parts of the republican set-up.

Catherine Nevin
Born in the same year as Willie McClean – 1951 – in Kilboggan, outside Nurney in County Kildare, not far from Kildare town, Catherine Nevin, née Scully, was the oldest of three children. Catherine's father worked a thirty-two-acre farm, her mother was a seamstress and the family lived in a small cottage on the farm. By all appearences, Catherine's early years were normal – at least for someone growing up in rural Ireland in the 1950s, during an economic depression.

Educated first in the national school near where she

lived, young Catherine progressed to Presentation College in Nurney, where she eventually sat her Leaving Certificate. This was an achievement in itself, given that not many girls in rural areas were given the chance to stay at school long enough to complete their Leaving Cert. It also paints a picture of a determined and ambitious young woman, although those who taught her find it hard to reconcile the Catherine they knew with the woman convicted of murdering her own husband.

Catherine Nevin's mother still lives in Nurney, while her father passed away in 1996, six months after Tom Nevin's demise. She has one brother, Vincent, who works as an engineer in Dublin, and a sister, Betty, who is married with children and works as an aroma-therapist.

Nothing has come to light that shows any early aberrant behaviour on Catherine Nevin's part. None-theless, whatever the cause of her transformation, by the time she had found work in the Castle Hotel on Gardiner Row in Dublin, she – or at least her priorities – had changed. Maybe this was due to her moving to the big city, or maybe it was to do with the fact that she felt she could express herself without first seeking parental consent.

The Castle Hotel was a hotbed of Republican sentiment – John Jones remembers meeting former IRA Chief of Staff Joe Cahill there – and it is possible that Catherine Nevin was carried away by the whole scene there. What is clear is that she used the pub and the contacts she made there as a platform; even when the republican movement split in 1969, she maintained contacts on both sides of the divide.

As well as the obvious romance associated with the republican cause, Catherine was attracted to what we might now call the 'X-Files' factor. Information was power, and she was already party to information that was of interest to other people. In the years ahead, she would gather her information from one source and dispense it to another to serve her own ends.

Allied to that is the air of impenetrability that surrounds some people who are close to the movement, if not directly involved in it. This is usually characteristic of family members of republicans and makes some feel untouchable – a situation that can cause problems. Catherine Nevin delighted in her republican connections and was not afraid to mention them when she wanted to threaten people. She made several trips to the North and gave the impression to those close to her that she was more heavily involved in the republican movement than she really was.

Catherine Nevin, although not a particularly pretty woman, possessed a certain charm and was fairly overt about her sexuality. This was like a beacon to some men, and she bedded many of them before – and during – her marriage to Tom. Whoever the partner, the reason for the liaison was the same – to get something from them.

She met Tom Nevin in the Castle Hotel in 1972. He was from Tynagh in Galway and was employed as a barman in the Emmet House in Inchicore. Ten years older than Catherine, he was already married but was in the process of getting an annulment when they first met. By 1974 they were living together in Mayfield Road and eventually married when the annulment of Tom's first marriage came through. The wedding took place in the Church of St John Lateran in Rome on 13 January 1977.

Before they got married, Catherine had left the Castle Hotel and had taken a course in grooming and deportment in Coleraine. She began to tour the country, going from school to school teaching pupils interview techniques, and she also gave advice on how they should carry themselves. When schools started to employ career-guidance teachers, Catherine wasn't needed any more. She then set up the Catherine Scully Model Agency and Beauty Grooming School. Although it fizzled out, this venture demonstrated that she was a woman of ideas who also coveted power and money.

The Nevins had greater success in the area of property, and by the start of the 1980s they had three houses, one at 446 South Circular Road, in Catherine's name, one on Mountshannon Road off South Circular Road, which was let in seven flats, and the house on Mayfield Road. The disharmony that developed in the Nevin household has been written about exhaustively, but before 1984 there is little or no evidence to suggest that they were at each other's throats. But then, they were rarely in the public eye.

Tom was running the Barn House in Dolphin's Barn in the south inner city for his uncle until it was sold in 1984 and he was suddenly out of work, but it seemed that Catherine had bigger plans, and in 1985 they leased the Barry House in Finglas West. They sub-sequently moved from Mayfield Road to Greenpark in Clondalkin. It is significant that it was now Catherine who made all the running. Tom, it appears, didn't think much of the pub, but he would have been persuaded that it was just a stepping stone to somewhere better.

According to John Jones, Catherine Nevin had definite plans to buy the Barry House; if the couple had bought that pub, she would perhaps have got to where she was most comfortable – among republicans. But it seems they fell out with the owner of the pub, and just over a year later they bought Jack White's Inn on the main Dublin–Rosslare road, three miles from Brittas Bay and about seven from the town of Arklow.

For Tom and Catherine Nevin, it was their dream home, but behind the scenes the marriage had already started to falter. Catherine was having an affair with Willie McClean – one which had started when Tom was still working for his uncle and finished about six months into their tenure in Jack White's.

Catherine still made the occasional trip up to Finglas. Whatever excuses she gave her husband for these excursions, he would scarcely have believed she was asking people to murder him.

2

AGENT PROVOCATEUR

After the republican movement split into two rival factions – the Officials and the Provisionals – men who had once fought side by side were now locked in a bitter and ultimately bloody feud that would continue north and south of the border against the backdrop of the Troubles. The Provisional IRA would survive the schism to spearhead the republican cause, whilst the Officials, or 'Stickies', as they were known, faded into relative obscurity.

In 1970, at the time of the split, Catherine Nevin (then Scully) was working as a receptionist in the Castle Hotel in Dublin, a well-known republican haunt. It is clear that not only was she influenced by the republican rhetoric that was being espoused by the hotel's patrons, but she was also courting both sides – a tactic she would use continously and with devastating effect for the next thirty years.

Just one year after her Leaving Certificate, Catherine Scully, an ambitious young girl from Nurney, County Kildare, was rubbing shoulders with the likes of Joe Cahill (of the Provisional IRA) and Cathal Goulding (of the Official IRA), and indeed she would later claim that both attended the opening of Jack White's in 1986, though this is disputed.

While the attitude of successive Irish governments towards the IRA never softened, the early 1980s saw a concerted effort by the establishment to snuff out the Provisional IRA and reduce the growing support for Sinn Féin, which had been at its highest level in decades after the hunger strikes. Known IRA members and Sinn Féin activists were placed under round-the-clock surveillance, phones were tapped, homes were raided and every attempt was made to suffocate the republican movement.

Those keeping Channel Vision, the TV-repair shop at 2A Church Street in Finglas which doubled as the local Sinn Féin office, under surveillance, would have noticed a well-dressed lady enter the building in the winter of 1984 but might well have surmised that she was going in to enquire about a television. Maybe they had sent her in there. This woman was Catherine Nevin.

John Jones
'My first impression of her was that she was well-groomed – every inch the businesswoman,' Jones recalls. 'She entered the office and asked for me by name, then introduced herself and told me that she had been into the [Sinn Féin] office in Blessington Street and had spoken to Christy Burke. He had given her my name and had told her to call out. When I checked later with Blessington Street and then Parnell Square, nobody had any record of her having called and Christy was adamant that he had never spoken to her.'

Jones would not be able to check out her claim until after she had left, but the nature of her enquiry had made him suspicious anyway. 'She asked me which pubs in the area were available,' he continues, 'which I thought was strange. I mean, I would see the logic if she had already bought or leased a pub and wanted to be told about the community she was moving into, but here she was asking me about pubs in the Finglas area. I genuinely couldn't help her and, given that it was my business to be suspicious, alarm bells were ringing by now. But the truth is, I was so busy, what with the advice centre and the TV business, that it wasn't long before I had put her to the back of my mind.'

The next Jones heard of her, she had leased the Barry House in Finglas West, deep in republican heartland, with Tom. It is plausible that she would have been aware of the problems the pub had suffered before she met Jones, given that it had been the scene of a full-scale riot the year before – an incident that had made the front page of most of the newspapers. The pub's owner, Michael Moran, who also owned the nearby Northway pub, was offering the lease at a rock-bottom price. For the Nevins, who dreamed of owning their own pub, this was the ideal opportunity to prove to the banks that they could be trusted with a pub of their own.

'Not long after they took over the pub, she was back in and out of the offices,' Jones says, 'and offered to help us in any way she could. She allowed us to sell *An Phoblacht* in the pub, we had meetings in the pub, we ran fund-raisers there and she also asked us to supply the doormen, which we did. When they moved in, she also asked me to rig up the sound equipment and TV, and I duly obliged'.

Catherine Nevin's willingness to help the IRA didn't

end there. She told Jones that, if they managed to buy the Barry House, she would renovate the place, and she asked whether they would be interested in locating an arms dump in the pub. A false wall would be built in the cellar and the dump would be completely sealed off. Jones was keen on the idea but also wary, and when the Nevins moved on to pastures new the plan was shelved. (Not long after the Nevins had left the pub, a rumour circulated among the local community and the gardaí that there was an arms dump in the place, and the place was raided several times. This author suspects that those rumours emanated from Catherine Nevin.)

So why did Catherine Nevin approach Jones in the first place? The most obvious answer is that she was trying to ingratiate herself with someone she regarded as – or had been told was – powerful and influential. But then, nothing about Catherine Nevin's behaviour was obvious. Again it begs the question, was she an operative for Special Branch? Whatever the reasons, it was not long before the Nevins were a fixture in the Barry House.

'I have to say that the suspicions lingered,' Jones recalls, 'so I organised to have a background check done on her, and, well, it showed up nothing, but there was just something about her. Still, I wasn't going to be able to articulate [my suspicions] to anyone else until I was doubly sure.'

Tom Nevin stayed in the background at this time but was well liked by the regulars of the Barry House for his pleasant demeanour. Catherine, it seems, made all the running. 'She made every attempt to ingratiate herself with those people she felt were important,' says Jones. 'She even suggested that her phone was been tapped and that Special Branch were having her watched. She got to know the main players and their wives but had little time for the rank-and-file republicans. At this stage I decided that she was in the pay of either the Brits or the Branch and that she was trying to infiltrate the organisation. Certain republicans were told to be careful what they said to her. We knew that MI5 had a unit working in the general area and the impression I got from Jones was that he was nearly convinced that she was on their payroll.

'What disturbed us more was that Special Branch was all over us. Ordinary guys in the Cumann were continually harassed, and here she was organising all sorts of republican events, mouthing republican sentiments, and she hadn't been touched.'

One incident highlights these differences. A few months after the Nevins had moved in, Jones decided to organise a 'republican week'. This had to do with the politicisation of Sinn Féin, which was then at an embryonic stage, and the organisers were able to use the prisoner issue as a launch pad to draw in the disaffected. Part of the brief to raise money for the twelve Finglas men, including Gerry Heapes, in Portlaoise. It was a week-long programme, with parties for the children, fund-raising events, rallies and demonstrations.

The speakers included several top-ranking members of the Sinn Féin Ard Comhairle, and an open-back trailer was hired for the day, at a cost of about £5, from which these people would deliver their speeches. The fact that the man who had hired out the lorry had no republican connections did not stop the Special Branch from raiding his house and arresting him.

While all this was happening, Tom and Catherine Nevin sat on their car, parked just across the road from the monument, and remained there for the duration of the speeches. The Special Branch at the time was arresting people with the most tenuous republican connections and it seems strange that Catherine Nevin was allowed to go about her business completely unchecked even though she was openly courting members of the republican movement.

On another occasion Pat Russell was handing out leaflets when he was arrested and brought the short distance from the McKee Monument in Finglas village to Finglas Garda Station. Jones organised a picket outside the garda station, demanding Russell's release. It was a small picket at first, but the plan, if Russell wasn't released, was to hijack two articulated lorries and use them to block the North Road. Russell was released before any drastic action was taken.

'If I was to be honest, I think I got to the stage where I was being affected by the general paranoia in the locality,' Jones says. 'I mean, we were under an inordinate amount of pressure and the reality was there was no further penetration. I formed the opinion that she was no more than a glorified name-dropper. She was very shrewd, though, always in control – I'll give her that.'

Like the other two solicitees, Jones received an invitation to the opening of Jack White's but, unlike the others, he turned the offer down. 'I didn't have any feelings about the woman one way or the other,' he recalls, 'but I was a busy man with a growing family and I didn't have the time or the desire to be traipsing down the country to attend a party. I thought I'd seen the last of her but her visits to the office resumed and it seemed odd, although I didn't make much of it at the time.'

She then proposed that she could act as a traveller for the IRA. Nobody would stop and question her, she told Jones, because she looked much too respectable. She could carry information or whatever needed to be carried to whatever country it needed to be carried to. If she hadn't been so serious about it, Jones would have thought it funny.

Jones had, up to then, turned down every proposal Catherine Nevin had put forward but he was eager to find out who was pulling her strings. On another occasion she offered one of the flats in the house in South Circular Road to the IRA to be used as a safe house for prison escapees and for IRA activities, or for whatever purpose they might need it. Tom Thompson agreed to stay over in the flat for one night a week to test her mettle. Within a few days she was back to Jones, claiming that she had entered the flat herself and had been set upon by two men with English accents. She told him that she suspected they were SAS and that she had tried to grab them but they had got away.

Now Jones was convinced that Catherine Nevin was a garda informer but he had to be sure, and when she suggested they meet up in the Mullingar House in Chapelizod he asked two men to follow her. They would tail Catherine Nevin once she left the meeting.

'She told me she had a great idea,' says Jones. 'That it would be a great coup for the IRA if they could photograph a garda in a compromising position. She would arrange for the garda to be in the flat in South Circular Road, and we would set up the flat so that a photograph could be taken. Then she suggested we blackmail him to find out what information the gardaí had on the IRA.' Given that several witnesses at the trial had testified that they had observed Inspector Tom Kennedy enter and leave the flat on several occasions, we can only assume that she was talking about him.

The two men detailed to follow Catherine Nevin wish to remain anonymous but have agreed to tell their story. Sinn Féin Member One described how they followed her from the pub over to the flats and then to the Mater Private Hospital. 'From there we followed her into town and then out in the direction of Jack White's,' he recalls. 'On the way she stopped off at another pub. I can't remember the name. She went inside and we waited for about five minutes outside before I told [Sinn Féin Member Two] to go in and see what he could see.'

'When I went into the pub,' recalls the second man, 'I could see her straight away sitting with a fella who had his back turned to me. I waited until he got up to go to the bar and then I recognised him as Special Branch. I had to get out of there fast before he recognised me.' It confirmed all Jones's suspicions.

Jones said in court that he thought she was working for the gardaí. This wasn't strictly true, however: he knew for a fact she was working for them but he had figured that there was no doubt that Catherine Nevin's barrister, Patrick McEntee, would ask him to elaborate and he would not have been able to do so in court.

Catherine Nevin was still a regular fixture in the Sinn Féin office but as far as Jones was concerned her focus was becoming more personal and less IRA-oriented. Although she didn't make any kind of advance to him, she began to shower him with gifts. It started with a basket covered in shells that she bought for him in the Canaries. Jones figured that it must have cost her some money, but that didn't save it from its final destination – the bin. Then she called to his house in Balbriggan, saying she had been to Dundalk to collect meat for the pub. She showed him the meat but he thought it strange that she would travel so far just for that. This author has discovered that Tom had always collected the meat and had got it either from Slaney Meats in Wexford or from Kepak in Meath. She gave some of the meat to Jones before leaving, and again the gift found its way into the bin.

When Jones and his family decided to take a holiday abroad, they called into Jack White's on the way to Rosslare and on the way back to Dublin from Rosslare. On the first visit, Catherine Nevin brought him around the pub and told him of her plans. 'She was going to make it a Grade A truck-stop,' he recalls. 'There was an airstrip owned and used by the Japanese and she wanted to tap into that. The European Golf Club was nearby too and she was eyeing that trade as well. She told me about the many European grants that were available because she was on the primary route from Dublin to Rosslare. She certainly knew her stuff and it has to be said that she was very innovative and forward-thinking.' Another time she brought up a convector oven that she had just bought that was capable of heating forty plates of pre-cooked and wrapped food in minutes. Why she was showing it to him, he couldn't fathom.

Again she suggested an arms dump for Jack White's. This time she showed him where they would build a false wall, but Jones dismissed the idea out of hand.

Catherine Nevin was enthusiastic about cultivating the local Protestant population too, and Jones did not object to that. And still the visits to the Sinn Féin office continued. 'She would ask advice about the business,' Jones remembers. 'I mean, what the hell would I know about the bar trade – nothing. I can remember her telling me that [Judge] Ó Buachalla was advising her as a solicitor. She talked and talked about this fellow Ó Buachalla and said he was a brilliant solicitor but I wasn't impressed and when she saw that I wasn't impressed she started going on about his father who had supposedly held some major position but it still didn't register who he was. It was mostly small talk, or rather *she* talked and I listened and listened and then I would turn off completely, just nod my head every so often. It got to the stage that I would ring ahead to the office and have a coded conversation with Tom Thompson, and if she was there waiting for me, he would tell me in code to stay away. There was no reason for her visits and I was just switching off, anyway. It didn't feel like she was building up to something – she would just drone on and on and on.'

One of the many details offered by Catherine Nevin

in her testimony relating to her involvement with the IRA was the story of the Killinarden Inn in Tallaght. Her version is that she and Tom proposed to buy the pub and that they were approached by the republican movement to front the pub for them. She also stated that the IRA planned to put up some of the money for the purchase and that money had come from the North and was being handled by Jones. Moreover, they had met with several well-known republicans to discuss the deal. She was quick to add that it was her husband, Tom, who was making all the running with the IRA, and not her.

So what is the truth about the Killinarden Inn? One thing is for certain: it has been a major source of embarassment for the IRA, and the man that Nevin said was responsible for the deal – John Jones – categorically denies that there was any such meeting or deal. A trawl of other republican contacts did not reveal the truth of the matter but at least offered enough information for a theory to be postulated about it. In the first place, it is clear that the IRA have several pubs in the Dublin area where they have entered into arrangements with legitimate business people. Secondly, the IRA had planned to buy the Killinarden Inn, had the money put aside to do so and were hoping to enter into an agreement with an interested party. Catherine Nevin had also decided, independently, to look into buying the same pub, and it was made known to her by someone in the movement that the IRA already had an interest there. If this was the case then it would be a major source of embarrassment for the IRA – that one of its members would divulge such information –

and to Catherine Nevin, of all people.

Aware that the IRA would be looking for someone to front the pub, Nevin threw her hat into the ring and pursued the matter energetically, even organising a meeting with some high-ranking republicans that may or may not have included John Jones and John Noonan. The meeting was an attempt to suss her out rather than the other way around, but it has become another source of annoyance for the IRA. One thing is crystal-clear: Tom Nevin had no part in any of the deliberations and probably had no idea what his wife was up to.

Willie McClean
Behind every Catherine Nevin lie there is always a grain of truth. When she was questioned in court about her involvement with Willie McClean, she said, 'I only know what my husband told me. He said he had plates and was into making twenty-pound notes.' This claim, which the state dismissed as being completely without foundation, was calculated to add weight to her revelation that Tom Nevin had been a member of the IRA and was well-informed on the murky goings-on of the Dublin underworld.

The truth, of course, is that Tom was not a member of the IRA, nor had he any associates in the criminal fraternity. But the claim about the plates is true. McClean had plates but they were for twenty-dollar bills, and this is the reason Catherine Nevin sought him out in the first place. He remembers their first meeting vividly.

'It was in late January, early February 1985 if my memory serves me right,' McClean recalls, 'and about eight o'clock in the evening, and I was sat at the bar in the Red Cow. In walks this one with a big fur coat, dripping with jewellery, and she comes straight up and sits beside me and we just got chatting. "I know you from somewhere," she said, and then we made our introductions. She told me about Tom – that he was working in Dolphin's Barn for his uncle and that she had just dropped him off. She was comin' on to me like you wouldn't believe and eventually she asked me back to her house. [The Nevins were now living at 367 Green Park Estate in Clondalkin, near the Green Isle Hotel on the Naas Road.] She was driving a red Cortina at the time and we went back to her house. After a few drinks, she got stuck into me and I've no doubt that I would have had sex with her on that first night but that it was the time of the month for her.' Catherine Nevin and McClean left the house at about 11.30 pm and she left him home before going on to collect Tom in Dolphin's Barn at midnight, but they resolved to meet again.

McClean had always suspected that Catherine hadn't just met him by chance but had known he would be in the Red Cow and had gone there to meet him. His suspicions were soon confirmed but he couldn't have cared less. 'About a month after we first met,' he continues, 'she told me that she had been speaking to John Noonan from Tallaght and that he had told her that I did "funny money" – that I could get my hand on some dollar bills or hookey sterling. Then just straight out she asked me to get her $30,000, which I did eventually, but the bitch never paid me for them. The worst part was I had known she was wrong from the first week but the sex was too good to pass up on.'

About a year after their first meeting, Catherine Nevin took McClean down to Jack White's to inspect the premises. She told him that Tom had decided to buy it but she wanted them to get a punter's view of the place. Tom travelled down too but in a different car, and he returned to Dublin almost immediately. 'The pub wasn't that busy,' McClean recalls, 'but it was a nice pub, I liked it. She booked us into a nearby bed and breakfast and I saddled her again. The next morning I left her back to Green Park.'

It wasn't long before Tom Nevin confronted him about the affair but according to McClean it was a very strange exchange. '"You're sleepin' with Catherine, aren't you?" asked Tom. "I'm not," replied Willie. "I know you are, and personally I don't give a fuck. I just wanted to know," said Tom. "I don't really care what you think, but I'd like to know who told you," asked Willie. "Catherine told me," said Tom. The thing was, there was no relationship to speak of. I know they were married and living in the same house but there was nothing there, so I didn't feel like I was coming between a man and his wife.

'The worst part was that I was worried about getting her pregnant when she told me that she had been sterilised in 1977. She told me but poor Tom only found out much later, when they were arguing, and he was fierce upset over it. He was a very, very nice man and even after our little chat we got on quite well. We used to speak away to each other without a bother. I remember him walking in on me and Catherine but he didn't flip or anything, he just looked depressed.'

McClean helped to move the furniture when the Nevins made the move down to Jack White's, and his relationship with Catherine Nevin eventually slipped into a routine. He would arrive in Jack White's each Saturday evening at about 7 pm and leave on Monday afternoon. McClean soon became a fixture in the Wicklow pub, sometimes helping behind the bar – but mostly helping himself to the contents of it. The routine suited him but Catherine Nevin wanted to see more of him and asked him to move in full-time. She was becoming very possessive too. For Willie, it was the beginning of the end.

By the time of the grand opening Willie was planning to break it off with her. 'Round about the August weekend, I started to pull back,' he relates. 'I mean, she was smothering me. When I did break it off she lost the head and threatened to have the IRA blow me away. Even worse than that, the following Saturday she arrived down to my house at the time in Kingswood Heights and told the girlfriend all about the affair. Needless to say, I was black-bagged and homeless, but I didn't give a bollix.'

The opening of Jack White's was significant too in that it was the first time that Willie met Gerry Heapes. It wasn't long before the two men were swapping stories of scams and strokes. An underworld source has confirmed that both men were engaged in a coal-voucher scam that cost the taxpayer millions of pounds. Today, the fuel allowance is factored into a person's unemployment benefit during the winter months, but a decade ago people received coal vouchers in much the same way as they were given butter vouchers. A social-welfare recipient gave the voucher to their local coalman and received the requisite amount of coal in return. The coalmen collected all the vouchers and sent them in to the Department of Social Welfare, which returned a cheque relative to the number of vouchers sent in. McClean, it appears, was getting the processed vouchers out of the department and giving them to Heapes, who sold them back to the coalmen at half-price. The coalmen in turn sent them back in again and were remunerated.

After the end of Catherine Nevin and McClean's affair, it was a further three years before the two saw each other again. In January 1990 McClean dropped into Jack White's for a bite to eat with his girlfriend, and Catherine Nevin seemed to be in great form. On his way to the toilets she took him aside and asked him for a contact number. Just to be safe, he gave her the number of his local, the Irish House in Harold's Cross, rather than a work or home phone number. Still, he did not expect to hear any more from her.

Gerry Heapes

During the eight years he spent in Portlaoise Jail for his part in an armed robbery on Leyden's Cash and Carry in 1977, Gerry Heapes honed his talent for woodwork. He made tables, chairs, crosses, harps – anything that might sell. When he was released he worked from the Sinn Féin offices in Church Street, drawing republican motifs on hankerchiefs.

One day not long after his release, Tommy Thompson introduced him to a woman who had bought a harp he had made in Portlaoise: Catherine Nevin. She was in the middle of her affair with Willie McClean at the time and at some stage after McClean and Heapes met for the first time the former took a particular liking to the harp, which he promptly stole.

Catherine Nevin was furious and immediately approached Heapes to retrieve it for her. 'She wanted me to have a word with him,' Heapes recalled. 'You know, stick a gun into his chest and persuade him to give it back that way, so I just pulled Willie aside and told him it was best for all concerned if he handed back the harp.' Willie obliged.

Heapes and his wife were invited to the opening of Jack White's but only arrived at about 11 pm, having lost their way and crossed most of County Wicklow. 'The place was jammed,' Heapes remembers, 'and once we arrived Catherine brought us around, but rather than making introductions she just pointed people out. There was a judge, a TD, a few councillors, farmers, wealthy businessmen – you name it, they were there. Later she claimed that both Joe Cahill and Cathal Goulding were there, but I didn't see either of them.'

Most of the republican sources the author has spoken to agreed that it is highly unlikely that both Cahill and Goulding were there, given that the Provisionals under Cahill were responsible for the death of Goulding's son and that the Officials under Goulding were responsible for shooting Cahill's brother. If either of the two republican leaders were there, it was probably Goulding, who was a close friend of Catherine Nevin for years.

Heapes and his wife spent the night in one of the many rooms in Jack White's. Not even Tom's family were extended that courtesy. They met Catherine the next morning as she left the bedroom she was sharing with Willie McClean and they were introduced to Tom too. He was, Heapes remembers, 'a big culchie but an absolute gentleman, very easy-going.' Anyone who had stayed the night was invited down for dinner the next day before they went their separate ways.

Three days later, Heapes saw her again. She told him some kegs had gone missing – that she had an idea who it was and she wanted him to go down to Wicklow to sort it out. He never did.

A few weeks after that, she was alleging that two men had broken into the flats on South Circular Road and had robbed two leather jackets, and again she wanted him to sort it out. 'To be honest, she was becoming a bit of a pest,' Heapes remembers. 'She was always dropping names and I had reason to believe that she was making up these stories because she thought I was someone of influence.'

On another occasion, in 1987, several IRA members were arrested during a training exercise not far from Jack White's and Catherine Nevin told Jones that, had she known about it, she would have been able to tip them off about the garda plan to intercept them. At a later date, when she suggested that she start to compile intelligence on the Wicklow Orange Lodge, Jones wondered whether she was greedy or just mad. He figured that she would try to court anyone of influence, regardless of who they were or what they believed.

She then tried a different tack. 'She told me that she was having a problem with some coppers down in Arklow,' Heapes continues, 'and she was going to have them done for sexual assault on a young member of her staff. "I have the person to do it," she said, "and then they'll know the power I have." The gardaí in question were Garda Mick Murphy and Garda Vincent Whelan, and these allegations have effectively destroyed the two men's careers.

Catherine Nevin would tell Heapes that she could get her hands on any information he needed, but he was more interested in getting money – after all, he had a wife and five children to take care of. He didn't have long to wait: soon she would be offering him money too.

3

SOLICITATIONS

Catherine Nevin, it seems, had always been attracted to people of power and influence. The opening of Jack White's was probably her finest hour: she had assembled people of all backgrounds, and she was the common denominator. At least, that's how it seemed to those whose friendship she sought.

Everyone agreed that Catherine Nevin was a bit crazy and certainly dangerous, though not a physical threat. Money and power both have a corruptive influence, and nobody doubted that she pursued both with equal vigour, but it would appear that they all underestimated her. When, over a three-year period, she solicited three men to kill her husband, Tom, she had to be taken seriously.

John Jones
'It was like she was trying to cultivate a friendship where there was none,' Jones recalls. 'She was making every possible effort to ingratiate herself [with me] and I couldn't understand why. I had passed on every proposition she had made and yet she was still coming back with more. What I can see clearly now – but didn't realise at the time – was she was building up to something.'

Jones and Catherine Nevin's meeting in the Sinn Féin Advice Centre on Church Street in Finglas had begun like countless others, with Catherine Nevin talking about everything and anything and Jones switching off. 'There was something on her mind,' Jones remembers. 'She was beating around the bush and we had just spent the best part of an hour talking about nothing. Indeed, if I remember rightly she was motioning as if she was about to leave, but something was holding her back – some unfinished business. The conversation we had next I will never forget. "I have a proposition," she said. "Go ahead," I replied, expecting her to come out with another hare-brained scheme. She started to rattle her keys and tap them on the table. "I want you to get the IRA to kill Tom," she said. 'I laughed and just palmed it off like she had just cracked a joke, and I couldn't believe she was serious. But I didn't want to believe it. She had obviously thought I was in a position to make it happen, but there were other people she could have gone to. I decided there and then that it was a set-up and all the old doubts about her came to the forefront. It was a moment of clarity.'

Jones was still mulling over the events of the day when he met his friend and fellow Sinn Féin member Pat Russell in the city centre later that evening. 'We had a meeting about some other stuff,' he relates, 'and I turned and said to him, "You won't believe what that headbanger Nevin's just asked me." "What? Tell me," he said. "She's gone and asked me to get the IRA to kill Tom," said I. "Ah, she's winding you up, John," said Russell. "She was serious – *too* serious, if you ask me. Something is wrong here – very wrong," I told him.

"Well, just be cool when you see her again, and if she asks you again, you'll know," Russell suggested.'

Jones spoke to another man that same night but he refuses to disclose this man's identity. It was Jones's opinion that the whole thing was a set-up – that she would be back, and that Jones would need to be clear in his mind about how he was going to deal with her. He didn't have long to wait. About three weeks later, Catherine Nevin returned, and this time there was no beating around the bush. It was a tense encounter because Jones was aware that she was going to raise the subject again and his natural instinct was to dismiss the proposition out of hand.

His duties as a republican, however, dictated that he assess her as a potential risk to the movement first and then, when he had worked her out, he could tell her it wasn't on. As far as he was concerned, she was a puppet for either the Special Branch or the British, and if he listened to her for long enough, he'd find out who had programmed her.

'Have you thought any more about the proposition I made?' she asked.

'What are you talking about?' Jones replied, playing dumb.

'About you getting the IRA to kill Tom,' she reminded him, with no show of emotion.

Jones remained silent and let her outline her plan.

'I can arrange to have £25,000 available on the bank holiday weekend. Tom will be taking money to the bank on the Tuesday after the bank holiday. He usually takes one of the young barmen with him but I can make sure he travels alone. The IRA would travel with him and he could be taken out en route to the bank,' said Nevin.

Jones says he cannot remember whether the bank was in Rialto or Rathmines, but his response was unequivocal. 'Not a fucking chance,' he said, his tone almost hostile.

'She had spent a lot of time programming herself and I could find no chinks in her approach,' Jones recalls, 'but I was convinced that she was trying to draw me out. I could see too that she wasn't going to let it go. If she was who we thought she was, then we didn't want to cut her off straight away. I mean, all she had to do was slip up once and she might give away her handlers.'

Over the next eighteen months, Catherine Nevin solicited Jones four more times: once at his house, once in the coffee shop near the advice centre and twice in the advice centre. The meetings were brief and unproductive as far as Jones was concerned; he decided it was time to pull the plug. When she solicited Jones a sixth time, he cut her off. 'I don't want the subject raised again,' he told her, and she never asked him again.

Indeed, she would never contact him again, and that suited Jones down to the ground. 'I had no interest in the woman, just the protection of the republican movement,' he remembers. 'When she stopped visiting, it was a case of out of sight, out of mind, and believe you me, I was glad to see the back of her. It was a very strange time.'

Willie McClean

His visit to Jack White's three years after the end of his affair with Catherine Nevin was significant to Willie McClean in many respects. Firstly, he was accompanied by his new girlfriend and was keen to show Catherine Nevin that he had moved on. Then there were the threats she made when they broke up about having the IRA kill him. His presence in Jack White's was calculated to give her the message that he wasn't scared of her.

Catherine Nevin was wealthy and influential too, and that made her someone to keep on the right side of, particularly if your calling in life is to relieve rich and influential people of some of their wealth without their knowing. But he was still cautious and, when she asked for his phone number, he was careful to give the number of his local.

Although she did not have his home number, Catherine Nevin had the number of his home from home, given his fondness for the drink, and when she eventually contacted the pub she found him easily. She was, she told him, in a private clinic in St Vincent's Hospital and would like him to come out to visit her because she wanted to ask him something.

'Well, like a gombeen, I went out to see her, with no notion why she wanted me there,' McClean recalls. 'She suggested first that we get back together, but I said "No, we've had our day" and she started to go mad, her eyes were rollin' in her head and twitchin' and I was beginning to wonder whether she was actually in hospital because she'd gone mad. Then she changed. She told me she wanted a job done and what with me bein' a mate of the General [Martin Cahill] and with all me contacts up north, she figured I was the man to sort it out for her.

'When she told me that the job she wanted done was to kill Tom, I told her "No way!"' McClean continues. 'She told me that Tom had a life assurance policy and that she stood to collect if Tom was killed. It reminded me of something she had said at the opening of Jack White's in 1986, when she said she'd have the pub on her own in ten years. I knew then she was serious and I just walked straight out of there with her screamin' after me,' he continued.

Willie McClean was taken aback but not surprised by her request. When he looks back he says that he should have seen it coming – that there was a definite plan of action on her part that involved getting rid of Tom and bringing him back to reignite their old relationship, but the solicitation didn't exactly inspire confidence in Catherine Nevin's ability to cohabit with anyone.

Unlike John Jones and Gerry Heapes, McClean had no reason to believe that she was trying to trick him. No, he knew from the very moment the words came out of her mouth that she was deadly serious and that, if he didn't help her, she would soon find someone who would.

Gerry Heapes

If the soliciting of Willie McClean was abrupt, it was in stark contrast to the length of time taken and the number of attempts made by Catherine Nevin to persuade Gerry Heapes to kill her husband.

One day when Heapes was working on the door of

the Barry House, Catherine Nevin arrived and asked to speak to him. When they took their seats inside the pub she began to tell him how her life with Tom was hell. She claimed that he was beating her, that they were constantly arguing and that her life was basically not worth living.

Then she dropped the bombshell. She wanted Heapes to kill Tom and would make £25,000 available to him if he did so. Heapes told her that she would have to raise more money – that what she had offered wasn't enough and that he would have to check first to see whether her proposal was viable.

His immediate reaction once she had left was that it was a wind-up. Virtually every day some battered wife or girlfriend came in to seek his help. When he did help them, he was rarely thanked for it and some even turned against him, having made up with their partners in the interim. It had got to the stage that the local gardaí approached him and told him that they appreciated what he was trying to do but that he was wasting their time.

He took their advice and since then has lived by the motto 'Never get involved in a domestic'; he passes this pearl of wisdom on to new doormen. Catherine Nevin was no battered wife, he had worked out, so what was her game? He put the proposition down to a woman having one of her moods.

Heapes discussed his meeting with Nevin with a few lads in the pool hall. In court he referred to these men as Mickser, Redser and Tommo and claimed under cross-examination that he didn't know their real names. The general view was that he had reported back to people who were in senior positions in the IRA but was refusing to give their names, avoiding the possibility of drawing new IRA characters into the case. He still claims that he talked to these men but also adds that he was duty-bound to report Nevin's request to a higher authority. He would neither confirm nor deny that the two groups of people were one and the same.

Working on the assumption that Mickser, Redser and Tommo were real people, a trawl of republicans in the locality sheds little light on their real identities. It is possible that Tommo was Tom Thompson, who was a member of the local Sinn Féin Cumann and had introduced Heapes to Catherine Nevin in the first place. In addition, Heapes said in evidence that Thompson was a regular in the pool hall. Nonetheless, there is no substantive evidence to prove this theory.

At the end of their first meeting, Catherine Nevin and Heapes had resolved to meet again the following Tuesday. Tom had the car to deposit the weekend's takings on a Monday, so she had the car to herself every Tuesday.

Heapes made his own way to the entrance to the Phoenix Park at the junction of Parkgate Street and Infirmary Hill, where Catherine Nevin picked him up. They then drove past the Wellington Monument to a point where they had a full view of Islandbridge. She told him that from where they were parked they would be able to follow Tom's progress as he left the flats, then crossed the bridge. He was a man of routine and could be timed on his runs, then intercepted. Catherine Nevin stated quite clearly that Tom was to be shot, not robbed, and she also upped the ante. Heapes would receive £10,000 up front and the £25,000 takings if the shooting was carried out over a bank holiday.

Although he showed her no outward emotion, Heapes was shocked. He had worked out it was not a wind-up but he wasn't sure whether she was serious about having her husband killed or whether it was a ruse arranged by the Special Branch. She had every aspect of the crime worked out meticulously; he found it hard to believe she was capable of such cunning.

He would have to keep up the meetings until he found out about the set-up either way, so whenever they met he would find fault with her plan and she would have to go back to the drawing board. If she was being used by Special Branch she would soon become exasperated, but if she was serious she would just run out of ideas and go away. Heapes decided to stick it out.

For the next meeting he was taken to South Circular Road and told that Tom came by the house every Monday with one of the barmen and that the takings from the weekend would be in the boot of his car. From there, he would make his way to the bank in Blanchardstown.

A fortnight later, Catherine Nevin drove straight to the bank in question – the AIB in Blanchardstown village – produced a bank book in her maiden name and showed Heapes that there were several thousand pounds in the account. She told him that she had someone inside the bank siphoning money from their joint account into this account. Heapes maintains that she was having an affair with the bank official in question; in a bizarre twist, this person committed suicide just before the Nevin case opened.

Every time she came back to Heapes with more money and a different plan, he found fault with it. At this stage the ante had been raised to £45,000: this sum was a combination of the takings from the pub and a payment up front out of her bank account in Blanchardstown, with the balance to be paid out of the insurance policy on Tom's life when everything had quietened down.

Catherine Nevin's insistence that Tom be killed on a bank holiday weekend bought Heapes more time because there were only so many of them in a year, and when one passed uneventfully he had until the next one to delay her plans. In this way, he could easily string her along.

Giving evidence, Heapes testified that Catherine Nevin had told him that 'on a bank holiday weekend the money from Jack White's would be given to the police in Arklow. There were two guards there that used to keep it in their locker, and then Tom would collect this on Monday. If it was a bank holiday he would collect it on a Tuesday off the guards and then head for Dublin for the houses to collect the money, and then on to the bank.'

Heapes told Catherine Nevin he was unhappy about the insurance payment. How could he trust her, he asked. There were two policies on Tom Nevin: one a standard life insurance policy with Irish Life and the other a mortgage protection policy with Irish Progressive Life Assurance. The two policies combined were worth over a quarter of a million pounds.

Catherine Nevin suggested that, if she failed to come

up with the money, he would be free to shoot her, but Heapes told her that that would be in no one's interest. Nevertheless, the issue of money was not raised again. Instead there was a lengthy period during which she made proposal after proposal and Heapes rejected each one in turn.

Tom couldn't be shot in the Phoenix Park because he drove too fast, according to Nevin, and because, in the park's wide open spaces, there would be no opportunity to hem the car in. When she suggested that she give him a key for the flats in South Circular Road and that he shoot Tom as he arrived, Heapes told her it was a non-runner on two counts. The narrow streets were hardly ideal for an escape and, further-more, the door was half-glass and any assailant lurking inside would be easily spotted by someone approaching the door.

Heapes was no nearer finding out what Catherine Nevin's motivation was and he was beginning to think that she was just a bit crazy. She had given no indication that she was working for some other agency and, if anything, she was as eager as ever to plan her husband's murder.

Heapes and Nevin's next excursion was to Blanch-ardstown, where Nevin explained that Tom always arrived just before the bank closed for lunch but that, on the rare occasions he was late, he would proceed first to Kepak to collect some meat and then to the Grasshopper Inn in nearby Clonee, where he would have something to eat. He would then arrive back at the bank in Blanchardstown immediately before it opened again. Nevin drove Heapes along the route her husband took and showed him where Tom parked his car and at which table he ate his meal. She also added that she could make sure that he was late. Tom could then be shot as he left the Grasshopper Inn. She suggested a time for the attack, which was to take place after the St Patrick's weekend.

Heapes felt that there were too many 'what ifs' in the plan and told her it just wasn't viable. She countered by saying that she would go with Tom and would delay in the toilets. Heapes told her that getting the keys to the car from Tom would be tricky. She said she would have an extra set cut for Heapes and would walk behind her husband as he was being shot.

Shooting someone at point-blank range would almost certainly wound if not kill anyone else standing directly behind them, Heapes pointed out to her.

'Well then, I'll walk to his side,' she said.

'But you'll get splattered with blood,' he told her.

'All the better,' she said. 'It would look great, me covered in his blood and with him dying in my arms.'

Heapes was exasperated. He explained that, with the death of a man as upstanding as Tom Nevin, who had no obvious enemies, the spouse would be the principal suspect, and if she was put under pressure she might talk. Catherine told him that if they arrested her, she would make sure that she left the station cut and bruised and swathed in bandages. The press would have a field day and the guards would shy away from an interrogation in case they were implicated in any roughing up of her. She knew how to deal with the guards, she told Heapes; there would be no problem there.

Finally Heapes told her there would not be enough time to plan the murder and she resolved to meet him again to talk further about it but they would never talk again. Heapes was subsequently instructed by his superiors to stop the meetings because they were yielding no useful information; he was also told that the matter was going to be put to bed.

Not long after their last meeting, Catherine Nevin was approached by some high-ranking IRA men and told in no uncertain terms that she was not to approach any more republicans and that, furthermore, she was not to approach anybody or there would be repercussions for her and whoever she had contracted. Tom was to be left alone, or else.

Given the period of time that elapsed between the solicitations and Tom Nevin's murder, and considering how eager Catherine Nevin was to have her husband killed, it is clear that she took the warning seriously: it was a major blow to her plans. The warning didn't end her association with republicans, however, and she was seen by several people in the company of Pat Russell on numerous occasions. Russell, it must be remembered, was the one-time treasurer of the Finglas Sinn Féin Cumann of which Heapes, John Jones and Tommy Thompson were members. Russell argued in court that his relationship with Catherine Nevin was purely a business one, but their association with each other must have caused some consternation in republican circles, given Heapes and Jones's dealings with her.

How long it was before she asked someone else – a republican or not – to murder her husband, we will probably never know, but she obviously reached the stage where the IRA warning was no longer a worry for her. This point may well have coincided with the declaration of the first IRA ceasefire in the summer of 1994. She might have surmised that any interference in her plans by the IRA would constitute a breach of the ceasefire and that this was unlikely to happen over some Wicklow woman who wanted her husband dead. That would have given her at least twenty months to seek out a killer and plan the murder.

At around this time, Eugene 'Dutchie' Holland arrived on the Jack White's scene. Catherine Nevin not only had an affair with him but also almost certainly solicited him to kill her husband. It has been suggested that the solicitation precipitated the end of the couple's short-lived relationship. Holland had only himself to think about and must have seen the inherent danger in staying with her. If she was to follow through on her plan, he would be a suspect, whether he pulled the trigger or not.

The other possibility for Catherine Nevin was a renegade republican who would have had no fear of repercussion or who might have been on the run from the republican movement. Such a person would have thought nothing of killing Tom Nevin. In the mid-1990s the republican movement was fragmenting again. Breakaway factions without access to IRA arms dumps would have seized on every available opportunity to raise money to buy weapons.

The fact remains, however, that we may never know who killed Tom Nevin. Nonetheless, according to reports from the crime scene, it seems that Tom Nevin may have known who his killer was – and may indeed have known the killer well enough to feel comfortable with them.

The possibilities in this area are limited by the fact that Tom Nevin did not socialise much apart from in the pub. If he was killed by somebody he knew, it had to be someone who drank in the pub, or a person from Finglas or Dolphin's Barn who had kept in touch. Even if somebody was pinpointed as the culprit, there would be little or no evidence to convict them. The murder, though hastily prepared, has left no evidence of the killer. Nonetheless, most of the evidence in the case points to Catherine Nevin's involvement in the murder of her husband.

4

PAT RUSSELL

Apart from the deceased, only one man had kept in constant contact with Catherine Nevin from the early 1980s through to 1996 and the murder in Jack White's Inn. He was also the only person, apart from the accused, who had frequented the pub and who knew of Catherine Nevin's intention to kill her husband.

More telling still is the fact that he is a former republican who gave evidence in a state trial. Moreover, while his former colleagues John Jones and Gerry Heapes had been the pillars of the prosecution case, this man would almost come to be regarded as a hostile witness – not to protect the republican brotherhood but to safeguard his own business interests. This man is Pat Russell.

The fact that Russell was the first person to be arrested and questioned about his association with Catherine Nevin demonstrates that he figured very prominently in the list of suspects drawn up by the investigating gardaí. That he used subterfuge and deception in his dealings with Nevin comes as no surprise to those who know him well. The important question is whether he played any part in Tom Nevin's demise. The short answer to this question is 'no': there is no proof whatsoever to link him to the murder. Nonetheless, he still has some difficult questions to answer.

If Catherine Nevin had solicited his friend John Jones, and he knew what she was capable of, why hadn't he told Tom? Secondly, if he kept in close contact with her right up to Tom's death and knew of her previous intentions, did she give any indication to him of her plans this time round? Russell refused to answer these questions.

Russell would have been aware that Catherine Nevin had been given a warning to stay away from republicans after she had solicited Gerry Heapes, yet by meeting her Russell was violating this order. He might have argued to the powers-that-be that the relationship was strictly a business one, but matters were never that simple when it comes to dealing with Catherine Nevin. So who is Patrick Russell and what was he doing with Catherine Nevin?

Born in 1963, Russell was in his late teens when he joined Sinn Féin in Parnell Square. When John Jones set up a Sinn Féin Cumann in Russell's native Finglas, Russell moved his membership there. Russell, who is thirteen years younger than Jones, was a college student at the time and was seen as having an intellectual bent. His early contributions to the republican movement earned him the respect of the other members of the Cumann.

He was elected treasurer of the local group, and when John Jones decided to step down as chairman, Russell took his place. When Jones was solicited by Catherine Nevin to kill her husband, he confided in Russell: this was a measure of the esteem in which Russell was held.

By that stage, however, he had begun to drift away from his republican colleagues and into the cut-throat world of business. From humble beginnings he has become a very successful businessman, plying his trade as a financial consultant. Today, he is a wealthy man. Although he describes himself as a financial consultant and accountant, he is not accredited to any of the established accounting or financial organisations in Ireland.

This has not hampered his business dealings, however. He has had interests in at least four companies registered in Ireland and abroad: the Royal Irish Group, with offices at 11 Merrion Square, and its parent company, Royal Irish Financial Services Ltd, at 78 North King Street; Universal Management Consultants, an investment trust based in Jersey; and Garrard International Holdings, registered in the British Virgin Isles, with offices in Bolton and Liverpool.

The Anglo-Irish names of the first two companies were designed to open up business opportunities on the British mainland. But the fact that Russell was a republican makes the choice of those company names strange, to say the least. It is possible that he thought that his business might not do as well if his British work colleagues knew about his republican past; the company names may thus be an attempt to throw people off the scent.

So what was the attraction of Catherine Nevin for Pat Russell? Well, she had money, for a start, but John Jones felt there was more to it than that. 'Pat, like Catherine, always saw the opportunity to make money,' Jones says. 'He was always coming up with ideas they hoped to profit from. They would have made great partners too. At a time when she was still trying to ingratiate herself with the [republican] movement and was being kept at arm's length, it seems that Russell was her knight in shining armour.'

'But Pat was more than that,' Jones continues. 'He had contacts everywhere and, well, that suited Catherine just fine. He recognised, perhaps before any of us, that she was very egotistic and he knew just how to talk to her. He had her eating out of the palm of his hand. They were a perfect match.'

Although his regular visits to Jack White's only started in 1995, Russell had been seen with Nevin on several occasions before that. What exactly he was doing with her was a cause for concern among republicans.

Russell had by this time adopted the pseudonym John Ferguson; he explained in his statement to the police that this was at Nevin's request – that she was trying to change Jack White's accountants and she wanted to keep the details of the meetings secret.

At this stage, Catherine Nevin was putting great pressure on her husband to sell out his share of the pub, and members of staff at Jack White's have testified in court as to the ferocity of the couple's rows. Russell knew she wanted to buy out Tom – he said as much under oath – and he knew what lengths she was prepared to go to to ensure she would become the sole proprietor. Why didn't he stop her or tell Tom, or the gardaí, and break off contact with her? Gerry Heapes and John Jones had recognised the danger she posed and had pushed her away.

If anything, Russell's contacts with Catherine Nevin became more frequent. Bernie Fleming told the court that she would get a phone call from him 'once or twice a week, usually in the morning before Tom got up. After his call, Catherine would leave, saying she was going to Dublin or somewhere.'

Why the subterfuge? If the purpose of the phone call was to organise a meeting, why did she make sure that the calls came in the morning, when Tom was in bed? As he had never asked her where she was going before, why would he start now?

What was the purpose of the meetings? Russell had a simple explanation. On a date he thinks was 17 February, he met Catherine Nevin in the Davenport Hotel in Dublin, just around the corner from his offices in Merrion Square. She had declared herself unhappy with the pub's accountants and wanted Russell to do the accounts for her. He had told her he couldn't but had given her the name of another accountant, one Noel Murphy, of Pattney Murphy in Cork.

Murphy corroborated Russell's story in his testimony and stated that he had met Catherine and Tom Nevin on 14 March, when he dispensed financial advice. When Catherine Nevin told the court that the reason she had come up with Russell's pseudonym John Ferguson was to keep her dealings secret from Tom, however, Russell's explanation took a hammering.

Bernie Fleming, the cleaner in Jack White's Inn, also testified that she had answered several phone calls in the morning and that in each case, when she answered, whoever was on the other end of the line would hang up once they heard her voice. 'This would start about

8.10 am and would be over by 9 am,' Fleming recalls. 'This would happen on both the private and public telephones about three mornings a week.'

Who was ringing? If it was purely a crank call, then the perpetrator was an early riser who delighted in ringing the pub, waiting for the cleaning lady to pick up the phone, hanging up and then ringing again. In fact, it seems certain that, whoever the caller was, he or she was hoping that someone in particular would answer the phone and, given that Catherine Nevin was (a) one of only three people on the premises at the time, (b) the only one of the three people known to be involved in this kind of cloak-and-dagger activity and (c) the only Nevin with a reputation for being an early riser (Tom was known to stay in bed until 11 am), she seems to be the person for whom the mysterious caller was looking.

It seems strange that the mysterious calls and the calls from John Ferguson, aka Patrick Russell, both came early in the morning. That is not to suggest that the calls emanated from Russell: he had spoken to Bernie Fleming on numerous occasions and would have known she was only the cleaner.

What was the substance of the other calls? If Russell had established the parameters of the relationship between himself and Catherine Nevin in the Davenport Hotel, why did he continue to call her, twice a week. Russell gave a partial explanation of this situation to the court when he said that he had set up two meetings for Catherine Nevin with Noel Murphy and that she hadn't turned up for the first, so he had bombarded her with phone calls to make sure she attended the second, which she did. This still does not explain, however, why she dropped everything and left the pub after one of his phone calls. What was so important, for a woman whose plot to kill her husband was just weeks away from fruition, that she would preoccupy herself with Patrick Russell?

Russell told the jury too that he had turned down Catherine Nevin's request to act as accountant to Jack White's because she was 'a hard taskmaster'. If anything, from the evidence of Bernie Fleming, things were the other way around: Russell seemed to have Catherine Nevin on her toes.

It is obvious from the events that followed Tom Nevin's murder that the gardaí felt that Russell had many questions to answer. Russell would be the first suspect arrested for questioning in the Nevin case and, when the gardaí interviewed Catherine Nevin for the first time, Russell's was the first name they mentioned to her. She didn't reply.

I can reveal that, when both where held in Enniscorthy Garda Station between 26 and 28 July 1996, Catherine Nevin and Patrick Russell were brought into the same room by gardaí and were seated at the same table. The gardaí hoped to see some interaction between the two of them but there was none. This was understandable for Nevin, as she had something to hide, but if their relationship was purely business, why did Russell say nothing?

This turn of events might have been understandable if Russell had played the republican card, but he didn't. He would go on to embarass and virtually contradict the evidence of the only other republicans to take the stand in a case of this nature. His evidence was so pro-Nevin that the prosecution team were flabbergasted. His approach was smart too, however: by appearing to support her, he avoided the cross-examination of someone who could have done him real damage – Patrick McEntee. The esteemed Senior Counsel was hardly going to make things difficult for someone who had been nice to his client.

Russell left the court with his own reputation intact but he had made fools of his former republican comrades and had said things about the movement that will not easily be forgiven. In fact, I can confirm that the republican movement effectively washed its hands of him after the case.

Easily the dirtiest trick that Russell pulled off during the case related to his old Sinn Féin stalwart Tom Thompson, who had introduced Catherine Nevin to Gerry Heapes. Russell had told John Jones, who was looking for Thompson – in order to ask him to back up his early recollections of meeting Nevin in the Sinn Féin offices –that Thompson had died in Germany of cancer.

Jones was not in Finglas as often in recent years as he had been before and he accepted that Thompson's death could have gone unnoticed. Jones mourned his friend and even mentioned Thompson in the cross-examination, saying 'R I P' after uttering his name.

Jones found out after the case that Tom Thompson is alive and well and living in Blanchardstown. What had Russell to gain by telling one of his oldest and dearest friends such a lie? Patrick Russell refused to comment on this matter.

5

IN-BETWEEN DAYS

Catherine Nevin had chosen a career that was high profile – that of proprietress of a public house. Her position as landlady of Jack White's Inn made her a figurehead in her locality. Hardened drinkers were beholden to her, and the pub was a major employer in the area. Its position on the main road from Dublin to Rosslare gave it an added advantage.

The downside to Nevin's standing as owner of the pub was that, every day, her actions, movements, tempers and words were witnessed by several staff and customers. It is the careful piecing together of these fragments of information that help us paint a picture of Catherine Nevin's social life. Meanwhile, the testimonies of John Jones, Gerry Heapes and Willie McClean reveal something of the secret life of Catherine Nevin: her thoughts and her plans.

The greatest challenge for the prosecution was the fact that the period of time covered in the testimonies of these three men was 1984 to 1991. Tom Nevin was mudered in March 1996. What happened in the intervening years? With whom was Catherine Nevin seen?

Both Gerry Heapes and Willie McClean saw Catherine Nevin between 1991 and 1996. John Jones, by contrast, was glad not to see her during that time. Had she changed?

Gerry Heapes

'I saw her in Finglas a few times and she was always with Russell but we never sat chattin' or anything, just said hello and that,' says Heapes.

The first real contact Heapes had with the Nevins was on Stephen's Day 1994, when problems at home prompted him to ring up the Nevins to see whether he could rent one of their flats until he and his wife sorted things out. Heapes spoke to Tom, who told him that, while there were no vacancies at that time, two of the residents had gone home, down the country, for the Christmas holidays and Heapes was welcome to stay over the Christmas period in one of their flats. It turned out that he didn't need the flat after all and he moved back home.

About a year later, Heapes and a man named Pearse Moran made their way down to Jack White's to try to con Catherine Nevin out of a few thousand pounds. It was a perfect opportunity. Here was a woman who had asked to have her husband killed and was offering a sizeable bounty to whoever would do it. The scam was easy: take her advance, promise to do the job but don't bother. What can she do then? Tell the gardaí? Take you to court? Threaten you? Either way, the lads felt they were on to a winner.

When they arrived, Heapes and Moran planned to eat a round of sandwiches and then make the proposal, but when Catherine Nevin saw them she insisted they each have a steak. Before they had the chance to say anything to her, she started to tell them that she didn't want her husband killed any more and that the two of them had had a reconciliation. It seemed as though she had been tipped off as to the nature of their visit. The two men never even had a chance to open their mouths. They left for Dublin on full stomachs but empty-handed.

Pearse Moran was, for a number of reasons, an interesting addition to the list of prosecution witnesses. He was subpoenaed to court to back up Heapes's story of their visit in 1995, but at the time there were at least four warrants out for his arrest.

When, that same year, Pearse and two other men almost beat a drug addict to death in Tallaght, all three were caught. The other men, who between them had no previous convictions, are now serving time, but Moran showed up only for the first day in court before absconding.

Moran also made headlines when he was indicted in one of the most notorious cases of animal cruelty ever seen in Ireland. He received a six-month sentence for the cruelty he inflicted on his dogs; animal-rights activists were so incensed at his actions that they vandalised his car.

Irish Life retain Moran's services as a debt collector, and he has also made several television appearances when RTÉ News has covered an eviction. Most of his work is in the field of eviction, and he has been employed all over the country. He met Heapes when they both worked in Croke Park for Alan Gannon, who was also arrested at the same time as Heapes and taken to Enniscorthy for questioning.

Although Heapes had no further contact with Catherine Nevin, word filtered back to him about who she was dealing with, and he maintained a healthy interest in her movements. He knew about her meetings with Eugene 'Dutchie' Holland and other luminaries in the criminal underworld. The next he heard, Tom Nevin had been murdered.

Willie McClean
Willie McClean met Catherine Nevin once more, on St Patrick's Day 1993, when he and a nephew, bound for Switzerland, stopped on their way to Rosslare. The purpose of the trip was to collect some furniture, but with a long journey ahead of them they decided to eat in Jack White's.

Catherine Nevin was there and she came over to speak to them; she was friendly, if a little distant. 'We may as well have been strangers, the way she was goin' on, but I didn't care anyway,' McClean recalls. 'It was nice to know that I could pop in whenever I wanted and there would be no ranting and raving. She told us to call in on the way back – which we did, a few days later – but when we arrived she wasn't there. From that time until the taking of the depositions, I had no contact with her.'

John Jones
'Protection of the republican movement had been my priority from day one, and I felt that Catherine Nevin was a threat, so I went out of my way not to see her,' Jones says. 'I was glad to see the back of her, if you must know. I heard through the grapevine that she solicited others and I knew that she and Pat [Russell] were seeing quite a lot of each other but I hoped earnestly that I would never see the woman again and

I didn't see her up until the taking of the depositions.'
In 1994, just two weeks before the first IRA ceasefire,
Jones was hauled in once again by the Special Branch.
He was told that he was an idealist and that idealism
was dangerous. Officers waxed lyrical about the failure
of Castro's Cuba and of *Cosa Nostra*, whatever relevance they had to Jones's position. When they started
to talk to him about people who might split with the
movement, he began to understand their modus
operandi. What they didn't know was that Jones had
already scaled down his involvement. They then offered
him money to inform. He turned it down. When they
went to photograph him there was some orchestrated
jeering by uniformed gardaí before they let him go. A
week later he was again offered money to inform and
was told that they would pay for his son to be put
through college if he wished. The meeting ended with
a request for information should there be any change
in the direction the republican movement was taking.

Catherine Nevin
Although little is known of Catherine Nevin's private
life in the period after she solicited the three men, it
is clear that she had switched her interest from sub-
versives like Gerry Heapes and John Jones to the law-
abiding Inspector Tom Kennedy and Judge Donnchadh
Ó Buachalla. Pat Russell, Tom Kennedy, Eugene Holland
and her husband, Tom, were the only other significant
dramatis personae in the second act of the Catherine
Nevin saga.

Ó Buachalla is an interesting study. The accepted
sequence of events is that he got to know Tom and

Catherine Nevin for the first time on his appointment as judge to the District Court in Arklow. John Jones, for one, disputes this version of events. 'He [Ó Buachalla] was the subject of some of the conversations between Catherine and me long before she solicited me,' Jones recalls, 'and she used to rave about him – that he was helping her with this and that. You have to remember that he would've been only a solicitor at this stage.' If Ó Buachalla had ever considered himself a lucky man (he had good reason to think of himself as such, having gone bankrupt, only to be elevated to the bench by his old chum Charles J. Haughey), then he might figure that his luck ran out the day he met Catherine Nevin.

A judge is a useful person to have on your side, and Catherine Nevin certainly had Ó Buachalla in her pocket. How else can one explain the extraordinary lengths to which he was prepared to go to ensure that she became the sole licensee for Jack White's – and this despite the fact that she was the prime suspect in the murder of the other licensee. This was the incident that, in the wake of the Nevin trial, grabbed all the headlines. At the time of writing, it is the subject of an inquiry headed by Minister for Justice John O'Donoghue and to be chaired by Mr Justice Frank Murphy. Questions will also need to be asked about the behaviour of the judge towards the Arklow gardaí – in particular Gardaí Mick Murphy and Vincent Whelan.

While it was posited that Catherine Nevin and Judge Ó Buachalla had a sexual relationship as well as being good friends, there is little evidence to back up this claim. Nonetheless, it is clear that Tom Nevin saw Ó

Buachalla as a threat and did not like him that much.

Another principal in the Catherine Nevin saga is retired Inspector Tom Kennedy. In this instance, despite his vociferous denials, he and Catherine Nevin certainly had a sexual relationship, the effects of which on his own marriage have been aired publicly. Nonetheless, while it is clear that she was only using him because of the position of authority he occupied, there is no evidence that she persuaded him to act outside the law.

The fact that she would offer the IRA the opportunity to blackmail him spoke volumes about her real feelings for him, however. Although she named Kennedy as her next of kin on one of her many hospital visits, he represented merely a means to an end for her. It seems that both Ó Buachalla and Kennedy were flattered by the attention paid to them by Catherine Nevin and were blinded to her real motivations. Both have suffered from such lack of judgment and have sustained considerable damage to their reputations as a result.

It is clear from the events outlined in the previous chapter that, while she used the judge and the garda inspector, Catherine Nevin in turn was being used by Pat Russell, who had her wrapped around his little finger. It also seems that he was the only person to get the better of her before the authorities caught up with her.

*

In the aftermath of Tom Nevin's murder, the gardaí drew up a list of potenial suspects; towards the top of that list was Eugene Holland, or 'Dutchie', as he was christened by the media.

A couple of weeks after the murder, journalist Veronica Guerin was gunned down near the Green Isle Hotel on the Naas Road. Her murder prompted one of the largest and most wide-ranging investigations in the history of the state; it wasn't long before the gardaí had identified all of the principal people involved in the crime.

It is believed that Holland was the man who shot Guerin, but he found himself given a long jail term on a drugs charge instead. For a while, it seemed as though he had carried out the Nevin murder too. He had used Jack White's for a family christening, having previously bought a house in Brittas Bay, three miles away. He had been spotted with Catherine Nevin on several occasions.

Holland was eventually eliminated from the list of suspects but there is no doubt that Catherine Nevin solicited him to kill her husband too. In fact, she had a sexual relationship with Holland; this was a well-known fact in criminal circles. It has been suggested that he terminated the affair after the solicitation, smelling a rat. Holland would have been aware of Catherine Nevin's relationship with Tom Kennedy and must have known that, if the murder were to be committed, Kennedy would be the first to be dragged in for questioning, regardless of who had actually carried it out.

The long-suffering Tom Nevin must have wondered what his wife was going to do next – or how serious her threats to have him killed were. There is no doubt that he was hurt by seeing the endless stream of men that passed through his wife's bedroom.

Tom Nevin was under inordinate pressure to sell his half of the pub to his wife, but he held on to it. Why? What reason had he for staying? The best anyone can venture is that he was a proud man who was not about to be ousted from his own business.

Catherine Nevin, it seems, spent the intervening years trying to organise her husband's death. Whether she was constantly soliciting people to kill Tom and being knocked back by each of them in turn is not clear, but it is possible, given her reputation, that she was regarded as something of a liability. As she settles down now in prison and sees the years she has yet to serve stretch out in front of her, she may be tempted to offer up the name of Tom's killer; this possibility would not have been lost on those she solicited.

All roads were leading to the early hours of 19 March 1996 and the demise of a 'gentle giant' at the behest of his wife.

6

REACTION

For Gardaí Martin McAndrew and Paul Cummiskey, both stationed in Arklow Garda Station, the morning of Tuesday 19 March 1996 was to be stressful one. They arrived at the murder scene at 4.45 am, in response to an alarm activation, to find the car park empty and the door leading to the live-in section of the pub slightly ajar. Once inside, they discovered Catherine Nevin trussed up, with her mouth gagged. When they removed the gag, she began to rant about 'a man with a knife and a hood over his head' who had stormed into her room, looking for her jewellery. Then she began to ask for her husband.

While Garda Cummiskey tried to comfort her, Garda McAndrew started a search of the premises, entering her private bedroom first in case the assailant was still on the premises. The room was untidy but there was no sign of anybody there. He came back down the stairs to check the rest of the pub and noticed a trail of jewellery leading from the hall into the lounge and on into the bar. The light in the bar was on and the door to the kitchen was open.

What Garda McAndrew saw next will probably haunt him for the rest of his life. Even from the other side of the kitchen, the garda could see that Tom Nevin, whom he had known, was dead. McAndrew saw that Tom was motionless, that he was lying in a pool of his own blood and that his face was deathly white. When he drew nearer to the body, he noticed a gaping wound on the right side of Tom's chest.

Tom was lying on his back, his right arm outstretched and the pen he had used to tot up the takings still in his hand. The garda knew there was nothing that could be done for him but he checked for a pulse nonetheless. McAndrew would have realised there and then that he was standing in the middle of a murder scene and that it had to be preserved: every hair, every footprint and anything that might have left a DNA fingerprint now constituted evidence.

The most significant contribution the garda would make in the hunt for Tom Nevin's killer, or killers, was that he could detect no smell of gunpowder (Catherine Nevin had claimed the killer had had a gun), just the smell of gas. A fifteen-year veteran in Arklow and a participant in countless refresher courses in the use of firearms, Garda McAndrew knew what he was talking about.

An hour after the gardaí had arrived, the pub was overrun by detectives, a doctor and ambulance crew and the most senior garda in attendance, Superintendent Jeremiah P. Flynn. Catherine Nevin was interviewed at length about her version of events. By the time she had finished, at 8 am, the news of Tom's murder was being announced on national radio – and was being described as a botched robbery.

It would take a while for word of the killing to spread; later in the evening there were at least four men living in Dublin who knew that the incident had been no botched robbery but premeditated murder.

John Jones

Although his years in the Sinn Féin office in Finglas had been the most testing of his life, John Jones missed both the camaraderie there and the cat-and-mouse games he and his friends had played with the Special Branch. He was now driving a shuttle bus at the airport and, while the job made little use of his intellect, it paid the bills and he could afford to take courses in alarm installation and digital- and terrestrial-TV transmission. Soon he would be his own boss again.

The nineteenth of March 1996 had been a typical day at the airport, and when his shift was over Jones looked forward to a night reading a book and listening to the radio. He might not have been as politically active as he once was but he still kept abreast of current affairs and in particular the events that were unfolding in Northern Ireland. As he sat down to watch the early-evening news, he could hardly have imagined that the first news item would change his life forever.

'A man had been shot,' read the newscaster.

'Interesting,' thought Jones. 'I wonder who that was?'

'At Jack White's pub near Brittas Bay in Wicklow,' the newcaster continued.

In an instant, Jones was aware of what had happened and why. The events of six years before were replayed in his head. 'Will you kill my husband,' she had asked; now Tom Nevin was dead. It was a mistake. It had to be a mistake. Maybe it was a botched robbery. Maybe she had nothing to do with it, he told himself, but in his heart of hearts he knew the truth. As the newscaster gave more information about the supposed robbery, he knew that she had at last got somone to shoot Tom.

If he had told the gardaí all those years ago, maybe Tom would still be alive, Jones said to himself, but then, when he thought about it a little more, he knew this hadn't been an option.

Trying hard to grasp the news, he remembered that this woman, who had organised the murder of her husband, had once sat in the very room he was in now.

He thought about ringing the guards there and then, but he was a republican and republicans didn't help the gardaí with their enquiries. Feck it, those days of cloak and dagger were gone. They were in the past. An innocent man had been shot and he knew the reason why, and who had done it.

Then he gathered himself and began to recover some of his composure. He decided that he would have to seek advice on how to approach the guards but, all things considered, he still wanted to go down to the station in his home town of Balbriggan and tell them everything. He was determined that Catherine Nevin would pay for what she had done.

He slept fitfully that night, and in work the following day the killing was all he could think about. Still, at least he had time to think – time to decide what he was going to do.

Who could he turn to? He had considered going straight to the powers-that-be in the republican movement, but then he realised that those who had been briefed all those years before would have made the connection too and would be dead set against the movement becoming involved in the investigation in any way. He needed to talk to someone who understood the implications of the murder but who was not in a position to order him not to get involved in it.

In the end his old friend Pat Russell seemed the perfect choice. Jones had told Russell about the solicitation all those years ago and the latter was now a businessman and was no longer part of the republican movement. Jones rang the offices of the Royal Irish Group in Merrion Square and spoke briefly to Russell. Rather than talk about the killing over a landline, Jones decided to go to the offices in person to discuss the matter with his old friend.

The two men talked at length about the murder and about Catherine Nevin, and Jones told Russell that he was considering going to the gardaí with what he knew. Russell told him he was foolish. He reminded him of how the guards worked.

'You go in and tell them what you know and, wait'll you see, you become their number one murder suspect,' said Russell. 'That's the way they work. I'm telling you, they're not going to believe that some Provo is going to walk in off the street and enlighten them without there being more to it. They'll put it down to a guilty conscience.'

'But I have a guilty conscience,' Jones replied.

'But why? There's nothing you could have done, and that guilty conscience will get you locked up, mark my words.'

'I can't just sit back and see an innocent man's murder go unpunished,' Jones retorted. 'I have to say something. Some things are more important . . . '

'Like what? The murder of a man you only half knew.

I don't think the republican movement are going to see it that way.'

'I have to do something, Pat. I just wouldn't be able to live with myself if Catherine got away with it.'

'She won't, don't you worry,' Russell said, reassuring his friend. 'The gardaí are on the ball. They'll get to the bottom of it, and if they're as good as I think they are, it won't be long before you get a visit, and then, if you want to tell them everything, you can go right ahead, but make sure you get some sort of immunity. Somebody is gonna get done for this. Just make sure it's not you.'

'I think you're right. Better they get in touch with me, and at least then I can deal with them on my own terms.'

Jones was aware that Russell had had some contact with Catherine Nevin but was unaware how frequent – and how recent – their meetings had been. He now thinks that this coloured Russell's advice to him – that maybe Russell was only looking out for himself. If he had it all to do again, he thinks he would have gone straight to the garda station and told them everything.

As it was, Jones waited for the guards to come to him. They did, eventually.

Gerry Heapes

As the crow flies, Gerry Heapes's bedroom in his house on Harristown Lane was about fifty metres from the fence that encircles Dublin Airport and probably a further fifty from the point on the runway where the giant 747s power up their engines before taking off. He was lucky, amid all the noise, to hear the ringing of the phone through which he would hear the awful news of what had occurred in Jack White's the night before.

Heapes's initial reaction to the news of the murder was one of shock, together with the growing realisation that he was likely to be in the frame for the murder. The guards hadn't much time for him, he figured, and while he felt bad for Tom and his family, the thought of helping the enquiry never crossed his mind.

As far as he was concerned, he had done as much as he could by reporting back to his superiors every detail of his meetings with Catherine Nevin. The matter had then been taken out of his hands and Catherine Nevin had been warned off. Heapes feels that, if Tom Nevin had been told at the time about his wife's solicitations, he would not have believed that she was capable of doing such a thing. He had taken every type of abuse imaginable, Heapes reasoned; what difference would a death threat have made?

Telling the guards was again a non-starter. Apart from the obvious problems such a move would cause the republican movement, Heapes felt there wasn't a garda in the country who would believe his story. He knew the gardaí would trawl through Catherine Nevin's past and draw up a list of suspects; Heapes's name would feature somewhere near the top of that list. He was beginning to rue the visit he had made with Pearse Moran to try to swindle Catherine Nevin.

In the days after the murder, Heapes wondered whether the guards had any idea of Catherine Nevin's guilt. Under pressure to give them a few suspects, she might point the finger at him, Heapes thought. Sure, he could counter with an account of her solicitations, but who would they believe: him, the convicted IRA man, or her, the landlady of a respectable establishment with extensive garda contacts?

He knew they'd be coming for him. It was just a question of when.

Willie McClean

The reaction of Willie McClean to the murder was less circumspect: 'Fuck me, she got him done after all,' he said to himself when he heard the news on the radio. He felt bad for Tom and began to feel a little guilty about the affair he had conducted with Catherine just under Tom's nose all those years ago, but those thoughts soon disappeared.

He knew the gardaí would be around to see him at some stage; he would cooperate with them when they called, and not before. He was not going to go running to them. In fact, he had no idea at the time that he would become one of the pillars of the case or that his testimony would become as important as it did.

He thought about Catherine Nevin and shuddered when he recalled that she had asked him back. Sure, he was the type to throw caution to the wind, but he figured he would have to be more careful about who he slept with in future. He knew she was serious when she said she wanted Tom killed but, that aside, he never thought she would go through with it.

*

No doubt there were others who were experiencing the same spectrum of emotions as Jones, Heapes and McClean. These people were probably cursing the day they met her and were waiting for the gardaí to come knocking on their door. The guards, for their part, had only just embarked on what would become a huge investigation. Although their instincts may have told them at that early stage that Catherine Nevin was the culprit, they did not yet have the proof to back up this hypothesis.

Catherine Nevin herself had offered several bogus conspiracy theories but the gardaí were duty-bound to investigate all of them. It was going to take some time before they would crack the case.

7

THE MURDER INVESTIGATION

Although there were already discrepancies in her story, detectives working on the Tom Nevin murder investigation had to give Catherine Nevin the benefit of the doubt. Her earliest statements were incoherent, to say the least, and with the shock that most spouses would feel in such a situation, what she had said on that night might well be ruled inadmissable later on in court. If this was all they had to go on, they were in big trouble.

Although the investigators were unhappy with many of Catherine Nevin's answers to their questions and were aware of the statistic that states that a high percentage of otherwise unexplained murders are carried out by spouses, the detectives working on the case had ruled her out as the killer at a very early stage. Nonetheless, some of the detectives had decided privately that she had been involved, and with every subsequent contradiction in her evidence that hunch seemed more and more justified.

Tom Nevin's funeral had been a grand affair, with Catherine Nevin centre stage, accepting the condolences of the local community and some local TDs. For some who had not attended, the sight of her walking behind the hearse, clutching a rose, was chilling because there was no sign of grief on her face, though she did her best to force it.

Catherine Nevin did cooperate with the investigators in the beginning and, while this gave them little or no help in locating the murderer, it did heighten their suspicions regarding her.

March 20, 1996
The day of the funeral. On the advice of her solicitor, Garret Sheehan, Catherine Nevin made a statement in the presence of Detective Sergeant Fergus O'Brien and Detective Garda Joe Collins. The detectives took swabs from her hands and face for the purposes of DNA fingerprinting and checked her purse; they found no money inside.

Catherine Nevin made two important contributions at this stage in the investigation. First, she told detectives that none of her jewellery was missing. This was strange, given the amount of trouble her alleged assailant had gone to in order to find it in the first place. Second, she revealed that, when she had let Sergeant Dominic McElligott – the last person to leave the pub that night – out of the hall door, she had Yale-locked and mortice-locked the door after him. She had earlier stated, however, that she had only Yale-locked the door.

21 March
Catherine Nevin told Detective Garda Joe Collins that, when she was trying to release herself after the robbery, she had picked up 'a funny smell, [an] unusual smell' and had 'thought the place was on fire, and the smell

went away'. This seemed to contradict the evidence of Garda Martin McAndrew, who had picked up no smell of gunpowder, just a gassy odour. Still, the smell might have dissipated in the interim; further tests would have to be conducted.

Catherine Nevin had been asked whether anyone had borne a grudge against Tom and whether she had noticed anything strange in the days immediately before the murder. She responded by giving a detailed description of around ten possible suspects. In effect, she was sending the gardaí round in a circle; nonetheless, it was their duty to investigate every possibility in case there was a glimmer of truth in what she had to say.

The gardaí were duly rewarded for their persistence when one of these alleged suspects, a former bed-and-breakfast guest who had been greatly maligned by Catherine Nevin, gave them a vital piece of evidence when he told them that Catherine Nevin had refused him a booking on the weekend of the murder.

23 March
Catherine Nevin told Detective Collins that her first estimate of the amount of money that had been stolen – £13,000 – was wrong and that it was probably closer to £16,550. When they asked her for a Z reading (which gives the total value of drink purchased during trading hours) from Jack White's on the night of the murder, she told them it would not be accurate because drink had been served after closing time and the Z reading had been taken at closing time so that, if the guards had raided the pub, there would have been no proof on the till roll of any illegal drink sales.

25 March

Catherine Nevin told detectives of a man who had stayed in Jack White's on the Monday prior to the murder. Nevin claimed that the man had allegedly spiked the drink of a young girl and then had sex with her. If any evidence were needed of Nevin's taste for fabricating stories, it comes in the form of her later claim that she had in fact spiked the man's drink to get information from him about the local drugs scene.

4 April

Members of the garda headquarters ballistics section gathered at Jack White's to conduct firearm tests in the kitchen where Tom had been found. The tests were intended to establish whether the gunshot could have been heard or smelt from Catherine Nevin's bedroom. They found that the shot would have been heard from the bedroom and that none of the smell would have escaped from the kitchen.

7 April

Former inspector Tom Kennedy arrived at Wicklow Garda Station and requested an interview with the investigation team. He handed documents relating to insurance claims for the Nevins' pub to Detective Sergeant O'Brien and Detective Garda Collins and then told them the story of the missing engagement ring.

Kennedy told O'Brien and Collins that Catherine Nevin had reported the theft of the ring in December 1993 and yet, three weeks before the murder, Tom had presented her with it. She suggested that he had spent months looking for it and, with the help of some criminal contacts, had finally recovered it.

Kennedy must have known that what he was telling his former colleagues was of absolutely no use to them in their investigation. The purpose of his meeting, whether he realised it or not, was to propogate Catherine Nevin's claim that her husband had had extensive criminal contacts. She made this claim at a stage when she must have sensed that the focus of the investigation was coming around to her and she wanted to throw her pursuers off the scent.

12 April

Detective Sergeant O'Brien and Detective Garda Joe Collins saw the name 'Gerry Heapes' and a phone number for Willie Adams in Catherine Nevin's address book.

29 April

Catherine Nevin was interviewed by the guards and was asked about a number of people, not least the mysterious John Ferguson. She denied all knowledge of him. Moreover, she claimed that Tom Nevin was murdered by a former member of staff who, she claimed, had been passing information on to criminal contacts about the layout of the pub and of Tom's daily routine. Catherine Nevin made a concerted effort to blacken this woman's name, to the point that she asserted that the woman in question had robbed her jewellery, even though she had told the guards that none of her jewellery had been taken. It seems that Catherine Nevin felt threatened by this woman, perhaps because the former employee was just as intelligent as she was.

Catherine Nevin then introduced two new characters as possible suspects in the case: an amusement-arcade owner and an angel-dust dealer who had, jointly, asked her to sell Jack White's. She had refused; she said they had then tried to intimidate her into leaving by killing her husband.

Another possible suspect materialised in the form of the head of security at a rave party which was to be held in a field close to Jack White's. Catherine Nevin had passed this information on to the guards, who had set up numerous checkpoints. She described the head of security as 'a wrong one' but, when she looked in her address book for his name, she promptly changed the subject and refused to give the gardaí the man's name.

This man was Alan Gannon, who, it seems, had had the misfortune to drop into Jack White's and tell of the plans for the rave to the landlady, who had been plying him with drink. To make matters worse, investigators discovered his identity and then found that Gerry Heapes had still been working for him at that time. Worse again, Gannon had told them that Heapes had been working at the rave. The gardaí regarded this as a genuine lead until they dug further and found nothing.

4 May

The pressure of the full weight of the investigation was beginning to tell on Catherine Nevin. She knew she was the number one suspect and told the gardaí as much. Nevin then fabricated a ridiculous story about a satellite dish that she claimed was stolen off the roof of the pub; she said she reckoned the dish had been taken by people from Dublin because they were into that sort of thing!

Throughout, she put herself forward as the innocent victim who was now having to contend with an investigation into her private affairs. She felt as if all eyes were on her, and she reminded the guards that she loved her husband and would never have had anything to do with his murder. The detectives investigating the murder found that hard to believe.

Then she introduced to the investigation the 'tea leaf in the barn' – an acquaintance of hers from Dolphin's Barn who, she claims, had been promised money if he could locate and bring to justice Tom's killer. During the course of research, this author identified three men who matched the description of the 'tea leaf' given by Catherine Nevin; at least one of these men would, if asked, have been capable of murdering Tom.

Catherine Nevin told investigators that she had paid for the funeral out of the account held in her maiden name. She said she wanted them to know that, just in case they later inferred anything from the fact that she had made withdrawals from her bank account.

Finally, she directed a vicious diatribe at the Nevin family. Surprisingly, she told gardaí that she had no need for the pub: that the Nevins could take it if they wanted and that she had her own money and investments. Given that she was consorting with Pat Russell and that he was acting as her financial adviser, did she invest in any of his hare-brained schemes? Does she have any offshore accounts, and is it possible that the killer was paid through these accounts? This is perhaps a matter for the Criminal Assets Bureau to investigate.

18 May
O'Brien and Collins located the reddish-coloured address book during an official search of Jack White's and discovered that Gerry Heapes's name had been scribbled out in both the front and back of the book. They also found phone numbers for John Jones and a car registration that they traced to a vehicle owned by Willie McClean.

26–31 July
Catherine Nevin, Gerry Heapes, Pat Russell, Alan Gannon, Brian Capper and Pearse Moran were all arrested under Section 30 of the Offences Against the State Act and taken to Enniscorthy Garda Station for questioning. Russell and Heapes eventually gave statements, although Heapes refused to sign his. Catherine Nevin said nothing.

16 September
The gardaí discovered that Tom Nevin had taken out an assurance policy on his own life with Irish Progressive Life Assurance Ltd worth over £70,000. This, together with Willie McClean's testimony, provides at least part of the motive for the murder.

4 December
O'Brien and Collins confronted Catherine Nevin with the evidence of the three men she had solicited: Gerry Heapes, John Jones and Willie McClean. She refused to

answer their questions and instead handed the detectives the number of her solicitor, Garret Sheehan.

*

When the investigation team finally studied Catherine Nevin's claims one by one, they found a succession of contradictions:

1   A period of twelve minutes had elapsed between the time she had activated the alarm and the time the guards had arrived, and she could not account for her movements during that time.

2   When asked by Detective Garda Jim McCawl and Detective Garda Joe Collins how much money had been taken on the night of the murder, Catherine Nevin had instructed them to look at the amount that was in the books, but she could only have known the full amount if she had seen the completed figures, and then she would have noticed the dead body of her husband right beside her.

3   She claimed that, when the raiders were tying her up, she could hear 'someone shouting' and 'a noise like a saucepan dropping', but if Tom had heard the shouting, it would have alarmed him, and the state pathologist had said that Tom had the appearence of a man who had not even had the time to become agitated before he was shot.

4   If Tom had shouted and been animated, as Catherine had claimed, he would surely have picked up one of the many knives in the kitchen and lunged at the attacker or even sounded his mobile alarm.

5   Catherine Nevin claimed she could smell gun-powder from her room; although she said she had not heard the shot, she asserted that she had heard somone shouting.

6   She claimed she had been asleep when the raiders had burst in, and yet she had heard shouting only minutes before.

7   At Tom's funeral, she had told Assistant Commis-sioner Jim McHugh that the odour she had smelt in the kitchen on the morning of the murder was similar to that of the incense in the church; the type of gunpowder used to kill Tom Nevin was odourless.

8   She claimed the raiders had burst into her room demanding her jewellery, but she had later told the guards that none of her jewellery had been taken and had then accused a former member of staff of having stolen it.

9   She had told Donncha Long, a carpet-fitter, that she was going to have Tom 'done' and that he was gay.

10 In Christmas 1994, Tom had confided in Pamela Flood, Catherine's step-aunt, that he was scared of his wife and that he couldn't leave her because she wouldn't let him.

11 From 1994 to the murder there had been several reported arguments between Catherine and Tom, and in some cases Tom required medical attention, but like the archetypal battered spouse, he blamed the injuries on a fall.

12 Catherine Nevin had told investigators that Garda Sergeant Dominic McElligott and Tom were still in

the lounge together when she had gone to bed the night before the murder, but she had earlier said that she had shown him out and had then said that he had let himself out. McElligott confirmed he had let himself out, but this was before Tom had arrived back from dropping off Frankie Whelan and Johnny Brennan.

13 She had not accepted bookings for the pub over the bank holiday weekend, telling those who made enquiries that it was full.

14 A set of keys for the pub was missing.

15 For the first time, she had not let the staff stay behind after the disco the night before the murder.

16 She had insisted on paying the staff by cheque; again, this was the first time she had paid them in this way.

17 She had ensured that Tom was delayed in getting to the bank, thus ensuring that the killer's bounty would have to be held over in the pub.

18 Throughout the day before the murder, she had been in and out of the storeroom, checking on a wash she had never put on.

19 She had drawn the curtains in the old restaurant at 9.50 pm – the first time that she had done so.

20 She had said the bedroom light had been turned off, when in fact it was found to be turned on.

21 She had said the raider had had a long knife, but she had then said it was a short knife.

22 She had said the raider had worn a hood, but she had then said he had worn a balaclava.

23 There had been no evidence of a break-in. The killer had either used keys or had been hiding (possibly

in the washroom) in the pub when it had been open to the public.

24 There had been no marks on Catherine Nevin's ankles, which suggested that they had not been tied with the intention of hurting her and that she had made no great effort to free herself.

25 She had said she was reading when the masked raiders had burst into her bedroom, but had later asserted that she had been asleep when they arrived.

26 Forensic tests showed that, if she had been reading, she had read no further than the first page, as this page was the only page that had fingerprints on it.

27 In spite of claims that the raiders had turned her bedroom upside down, a glass of scotch and 7-Up that had been on the floor was not disturbed.

28 When Gardaí Cummiskey and McAndrew had arrived, they had noticed a trail of jewellery across the floor, but the only fingerprints on the jewellery box were Catherine Nevin's.

29 If Tom had been shot in cold blood, why had Catherine been left completely unharmed?

30 She had said that her face had been pushed into the pillows on the bed, but there was no such indentation in any of the pillows.

*

What also became apparent was that, not only had Catherine Nevin planned to murder her husband, but also that she had spent years doing so. For instance, when she had masqueraded as a social worker to invade the privacy of Tom's first wife, June O'Flanagan, perhaps the most interesting question she had asked was whether O'Flanagan would put in a claim against Tom's will. This was in 1972, and Catherine Nevin was only twenty-one years old. It is possible, although perhaps unlikely, that she had thought about having her husband killed at such an early stage.

Whatever had happened in the interim, by 1989, murdering Tom was at the top of her agenda, and over the next two years, as we have seen, she made several attempts to solicit Gerry Heapes, John Jones and Willie McClean to kill her husband. She set about laying the groundwork for a defence in the event of Tom being killed and her becoming the prime suspect.

First, she established an antagonistic relationship with the Arklow gardaí. This was the O. J. Simpson defence: if the guards found any proof of her complicity in the crime, she could say that they disliked her so much that they had planted the evidence to make her look guilty.

Then in March 1993 she forced Tom, who did not drink to excess, to get help for his supposed alcoholism at the St John of God's Hospital in Stillorgan. This would lend weight, she hoped, to her claim that he led a double life and that, in private, Tom was both violent and subversive.

Catherine Nevin then made several reports of republican activity in and around the pub to support her claim that her husband was in fact an IRA man. She enlisted a former garda inspector, Tom Kennedy, to give her advice on the way in which the guards operated. He could tell her about the procedural aspects of a murder investigation and this would help her stay her one step ahead of the posse.

Catherine Nevin also used Kennedy to relay false information to the guards, on the assumption that it was better that this information came from him, considering his former position, than from her.

It seems that Catherine Nevin's overall plan involved having Tom killed so that she could take over the whole running of the pub. When she became a suspect in the murder, Catherine Nevin would say that she was the victim and that Tom had been involved in all sorts of republican and criminal activities. Why was he killed, the gardaí would ask? It was probably to do with his membership of the IRA, she would say. She would portray herself as the loving and faithful wife who had stood by her husband through thick and thin – from the pain of the annulment of his first marriage to his alcoholism – and had the bruises to prove it. Tom Nevin was a violent man, she would tell anyone who was prepared to listen, and the jury would agree that she was the victim and would send her on her merry way.

Catherine Nevin, it seems, had forgotten the old adage that you can fool some of the people some of the time but you can't fool all of the people all of the time. Her house of cards was about to come crashing down around her.

8

BREAKTHROUGH

Two months had passed since the murder of Tom Nevin, and no one had been charged. Some of the detectives leading the case, however, had no doubts about who was responsible – if not for the murder itself than at least for soliciting someone to carry it out. All the circumstantial evidence pointed squarely at Catherine Nevin, but such evidence would not be enough by itself to bring a case against her, let alone have her charged with murder. The case was going nowhere.

12 April
The breakthrough came when Detective Sergeant Fergus O'Brien and Detective Garda Joe Collins lifted some names and numbers from Catherine Nevin's address book. These included the name 'Gerry Heapes', which had a phone number written beside it. The name rang a bell with the detectives; this changed the course of the whole enquiry.

Heapes, it was believed, was a genuine suspect in the case, and detectives felt that, if he hadn't pulled the trigger himself, he was certainly in a position to have had someone else do it. Nonetheless, they needed more evidence before they could take him in for questioning.

The 'find' was enough to convince Superintendent Pat Flynn that a thorough search of the pub would yield more clues. Six days later he issued a search warrant under Section 29 of the Offences Against the State Act.

18 May

The search of the premises changed the course of the investigation and extinguished any remaining doubts that Catherine Nevin was responsible for the murder. Her address book was to offer the most important clue: when detectives examined it for the second time in as many days, they discovered that Gerry Heapes's name and number had been scribbled out on both the front and back of the book.

Heapes disputes this version of events and is adamant that his name and number had not been scribbled out recently but concedes that the fact that his name appears in the book would have led detectives to his door either way. The telephone number printed beside his name was not his own but that of his employer at the time, Willie Adams.

Catherine Nevin's bedroom would yield more valuable information for the investigating team when they discovered several scraps of paper. One of these scraps had written on it three six-digit phone numbers: the home and office numbers of John Jones and the number of another prominent Sinn Féin member who had stood for his party in various council elections in the Finglas Ward before Dessie Ellis became a successful candidate. Another scrap of paper had the car registration DIL 5206 written on it. Garda checks on this number threw up the name of Willie McClean.

The last discovery was of documentation which led gardaí to Pat Russell. Detectives who interviewed the staff of Jack White's would have taken note of the report of early-morning calls made by a John Ferguson; it was clear that this man, whoever he was, might become their number one suspect.

At the end of the day, the investigating team had plenty of leads and possibly a theory as well: that Catherine Nevin had solicited the IRA to kill her husband. The three principals had all been members of the same Sinn Féin *cumann* and at least one of them was capable of having killed Tom Nevin. Willie McClean's role, if any, in an IRA plot to kill Tom Nevin had not been established.

1 June
Gardaí arrived at the house of John Jones in Balbriggan to be told that he was at work in Dublin Airport.

23 June
John Jones was at work for Crossan Transport at the airport when he was approached by detectives, who asked him, 'Do you know Catherine Nevin?' He agreed that he did.

16 July
Detectives visited Jones again at the airport and, although he agreed that he knew Catherine Nevin, he refused to say anything else on the subject.

26 July

After detectives raided his Merrion Street offices, Patrick Russell was arrested under Section 30 of the Offences Against the State Act and taken to Enniscorthy Garda Station. Gardaí told him that they knew that he and John Ferguson were the same person but he denied this at first. Later he admitted that he was indeed John Ferguson but said that Catherine Nevin had given him the moniker and that their relationship was purely a business one.

Over the next forty-eight hours Russell was interviewed on several occasions. In the course of these interviews he admitted that John Jones had told him years before of Catherine Nevin's plan to kill her husband but that the IRA had refused to sanction it.

27 July

Having accumulated enough evidence to bring Catherine Nevin in for questioning, the investigating team wasted no time in making their way to Jack White's, where, at about 8 pm, they arrested her again under Section 30. She, like Russell, was taken to Enniscorthy Garda Station.

Catherine Nevin said nothing throughout the length of her incarceration; it was only when her solicitor, Garret Sheehan, arrived that she issued two prepared statements to the gardaí, the first in effect stating that she had nothing more to say about the death of her husband and the second alleging that she had been verbally and physically abused by the gardaí. At one stage, she was brought into the same room as Patrick Russell but the two did not communicate, despite the best efforts of the detectives present to ensure that they did so.

The first fifteen questions put to Catherine Nevin at Enniscorthy Garda Station related to discrepancies in the story she had given to gardaí on the morning after the murder. The interview demonstrates that the guards were convinced that she had orchestrated the murder. The next two questions were equally revealing: 'Do you know Pat Russell?' and 'Do you know Gerry Heapes?' She gave no reply to either question.

The gathering of evidence relating to Catherine Nevin's complicity in her husband's murder was at an advanced stage, but it seems that detectives were no clearer than before about who might actually have killed Tom Nevin. The next group of questions show that the gardaí seemed to be pursuing the line either that she was a member of the IRA or that she had solicited a member of the IRA to kill her husband. It seems that Patrick Russell and Gerry Heapes were the prime suspects in the case:

> Did you go to a man some time and ask him to stage a robbery where Tom would be shot dead?
> *[No reply]*
> A man giving the name of John Ferguson rang Jack White's pub on several occasions looking for you. On 29 April 1996 DS O'Brien and I asked you if you knew a John Ferguson and you said you did not. We now know who John Ferguson is. Why did you not tell us the truth when we asked you?
> *[No reply]*
> Will you tell us about the murder – the truth?

[No reply]
Are you a member of the Provisional IRA?
[No reply]
Are you a member of Provisional Sinn Féin?
[No reply]

28 July
Early in the morning the usual drone of nearby aircraft powering up their engines had the windows in Gerry Heapes's house vibrating but it took a dawn raid by detectives investigating Tom Nevin's murder to wake Heapes and his family in his home on Harristown Lane.

In an approach markedly different from that used on all the other suspects in the case, including Catherine Nevin, Heapes's house was ransacked. Although the house was thoroughly searched, nothing of interest was found there.

Heapes was joined on the trip to Enniscorthy by his employer, Brian Capper, his former employer Alan Gannon and a former associate of his Pearse Moran. All of the men had been arrested under Section 30 of the Offences Against the State Act. Capper was Heapes's boss at the time, while Moran was a former associate of Heapes who had travelled with him to Jack White's in a failed attempt to blackmail Catherine Nevin.

Gannon, who is currently head of security at Croke Park, was taken to Enniscorthy because he had spent an evening, with others, in the company of Catherine Nevin in Jack White's. That night, Gannon had provided the security for a rave in Brittas Bay, three miles away. He had initially told gardaí that Heapes had worked there for him. It turned out that he had been mistaken, however, and he subsequently remembered that he had in fact sent Heapes to work on the door of Samantha's on Leeson Street.

Heapes had been through this type of ordeal a number of times before and was fairly unfazed by it. He had no intention of answering any of the gardai's questions but he also knew that this case was going to be different from others in which he had been involved. Heapes was shown Russell's statement and, although it did not implicate him, he understood its significance: it had been given and signed by another republican.

The detectives made every attempt to get Heapes to talk but he had seen it all before. They tried to get him into a room with Nevin, as they had done with Russell, but the best they could manage was to have them pass each other on the stairs, and there was no eye contact between the two of them.

They then held an identity parade: a witness was taken to examine a motley group of men that included Heapes. Gerry Heapes is a big man, standing about six foot three inches and weighing around twenty stone, but standing beside him in the line-up was a man who was no more than four feet in height and had a fairly heavy build. The men were asked to do a 360-degree turn as the witness walked up and down the line but in the end she didn't recognise anybody and the plan was scrapped.

*

Jones received a phone call from Balbriggan Garda Station and was asked whether he would visit the station voluntarily to answer questions about Catherine Nevin. He agreed and arrived at the station at about 5.30 pm, where he was met by three members of the investigating team.

'We have a question to ask you, John,' said one of the detectives.

'Fire away,' replied Jones.

'Did Catherine Nevin ask you to have Tom murdered?'

'I've nothing to say to you. I'm leaving,' said Jones, getting out of his chair.

'No, John, you don't understand. This isn't about you, and we have no interest in the IRA. It's a criminal case but as far as we're concerned it's a civil matter. We need to know: did Catherine Nevin ask you to have Tom murdered?'

'I need to have a solicitor. Let me call my solicitor.'

Jones rang his solicitor, who happened to be playing golf at the time and felt he had had too much to drink to be of any help to his client. It was the advice of a local garda whom he trusted that prompted Jones to give a full statement. He was also shown a fax of the statement by Russell, who was being held in Enniscorthy Garda Station. Jones's full statement read as follows:

I am a member of Sinn Féin. Between the years 1980 and 1990 or so, I had a TV-repair shop known as Channel Vision Ltd at 2A Church Street, Finglas. There were two rooms at the back of the shop which I used as an advice centre for Sinn Féin. This was run by a man named Tommy Thompson, RIP, and myself. Around 1984 a woman whom I now know to be Catherine Nevin called into the advice centre. She stated that she had been referred by a prominent city councillor. I later checked with this man and he stated that he couldn't remember anyone like that. Her query was in relation to pubs available in the area. This I took to mean either buy or lease. This was a very unusual request at a Sinn Féin advice centre and my initial reaction was one of suspicion. I wasn't able to assist her.

Some time later I heard she had taken over the Barry House in Finglas. She continued her association with the advice centre. She also introduced me to her husband, Tom. They made the pub available to us to run functions and sell *An Phoblacht*. She developed a close relationship with certain members of the *cumann*. I am aware that they tried to buy the pub while they were there but they were prevented from doing so over some agreement with the landlord. She appeared to me to be trying to curry favour with certain members of the *cumann*. She attended rallies with Tom in Finglas. These were political rallies. Some time later, possibly 1986, they moved to Jack White's in Wicklow. She still called into the advice centre, possibly once a month. This was when she stated that she was attending the Mater Hospital, getting blood treatment or visiting their flats in the city. She later started calling to my house in Balbriggan. On these occasions she stated that she was returning from Dundalk, where she was collecting meat for the pub. On one occasion she even left in a present of some meat. I still retained a certain suspicion of her.

I believe in 1989 Catherine called to the advice centre and spoke to me in private. She said that she had a proposition that we might be interested in. She said that she wanted us to stage a robbery and in the course of the robbery Tom was to be killed. She said the plan was that it would be arranged for the Tuesday following the bank holiday weekend. She said the hit would take place when Tom was en route to the bank. She said that the amount he would be carrying would be in the region of £25,000. This money would be for us. She said that Tom went to the bank with a member of staff normally but she would arrange that Tom was travelling alone. She said the bank was in Rathmines, Rathgar or somewhere on the south side. I didn't entertain this suggestion at all. I told her that we were not into that type of thing. I felt it my duty to report this approach to more senior members of the organisation. I got in touch with them some time the same day and informed them of this. There were two members of the organisation at this meeting. They concurred with my opinion that this wasn't something we should be getting involved in. She approached me with this on a number of occasions and eventually I had to tell her that I didn't want the subject brought up again, ever. She never mentioned this to me again.

I believe the last time she asked me was about one year after the initial approach. Subsequently, I am aware that she approached two other members of the organisation with a similar proposition. These approaches took place before I left Finglas. The last time I saw her was when she called to my home about two or three years ago. I can recall an occasion, either before or after she made the initial proposition, when she called to the advice centre. She had bandages on both wrists and hands and she had a black eye which she shielded with sunglasses. She stated that Tom had beaten her up. She said that the Tom we knew wasn't the same Tom that she knew after the pub was closed at night-time. She said that the guards that visited the pub and drank with Tom were fooled the same way also. I saw the report of the murder on the TV later on the day it happened. I immediately suspected that I knew what had probably happened. Over the following days, I began to have a guilty conscience about this knowledge. I rang up a Sinn Féin colleague and told him I was thinking of going to the gardaí about the matter. I didn't want to see her getting away with that. I was advised not to go as it may be putting myself in the frame.

Later, Jones gave a second statement:

I wish to add that the only time I can be sure that Catherine Nevin mentioned being assaulted by Tom Nevin was the day she came to the advice centre with her hands and wrists bandaged and wearing the sunglasses to cover her black eye. She may have mentioned it in passing at other times but I cannot recall it at this time. On that day she came into the advice centre and sat across the table from me. She took off her glasses and said, 'What do you think of that?' showing her black eye. I could have said, 'How did that happen?' or something like that. She went on to tell me that Tom had beaten her. It was at this stage she said that 'He is not the type of guy ye think he is and the guards that drink with him would be surprised by it too.' She went on to say that she had to put up with the effects of Tom's drinking after the pub closed its doors at night.

During our conversation she told me about the big plans she had for the premises at Jack White's. She mentioned a truck overnight stop. She mentioned that there were EU grants for this. She mentioned that she was being advised by her solicitor. When she put the proposition to me that she wanted her husband, Tom Nevin, killed during the course of the robbery, and in other discussions with her, it was apparent to me the reason she wanted him killed was to take full control of the business. She mentioned the proposition to kill Tom Nevin to me on at least six other occasions at intervals over the next twelve months. The way she would introduce it was during the course of general conversation, she would say, 'By the way, did you think any more about my proposition?'

These propositions were always mentioned in either the advice centre or the pub across the road, where I would go for coffee with her if she had looked for me in the advice centre and I wasn't there. When she mentioned the proposition I knew that it was the proposition to kill Tom Nevin in the staged robbery. She visited my home about five or six times. On at least one of the occasions I wasn't there and she just left a message that she had called. Having been made the proposition by Catherine Nevin initially, I discussed the matter with two persons, one of whom was Pat Russell, another member of the local *cumann*. The second man was a prominent member of the organisation whom I do not wish to name. Having heard about the murder, I contacted Pat Russell about my concerns on the matter. I told him I was going to the guards about the matter.

In a third statement, Jones said that:

On the night of 18 March 1996 and the morning of 19 March 1996, I cannot recall exactly where I was. I will check with my workplace to establish if I was working or not. In relation to the time Mrs Catherine Nevin called to the advice centre in Finglas that she had a black eye and her wrists bandaged – she stated that she had been assaulted by her husband, Tom Nevin, and she had attended the Mater Private Hospital. I cannot say exactly when this was but it was definitely during her time at Jack White's. As close as I can come to the actual time is to say it was between 1986 and 1989.

In his statements, Jones had told detectives how he had met Catherine Nevin and, without going into the details of her plots to involve the IRA in the planned murder of her husband, he took them through the various solicitations she had made. It was the report of her arrival in bandages on one of these occasions that sparked the most interest among the gardaí, however. If they could match the meeting with a visit to the hospital, then it gave his statement some validity, and at last they had a case. Also of interest was the mention made of her solicitor during the period 1986-9; although the solicitor's name is not given in the statement, Jones is adamant that it was Judge Donncha Ó Buachalla, then a solicitor. This contradicts the judge's assertion that he got to know the Nevins only after his move to the Wicklow area.

29 July
Gerry Heapes only once lost his cool during his incarceration – when one of the gardaí made the mistake of threatening one of his daughters. Heapes then flew into a rage, smashing one of the windows in the station, and was brought back to his cell. When senior officers heard of the threat through Heapes's solicitor, they were appalled, and the offending garda was removed from the premises – though not before they had taunted him once more, in his cell.

30 July

Gerry Heapes and Brian Capper were released without charge and, with only one train ticket between them to get back to Dublin, they entered the train station, hoping to do some sort of deal with the ticket inspector. They then discovered that he was the short man who had taken part in the line-up, and he was only too happy to oblige.

31 July

Heapes returned to Enniscorthy to make a statement, having got clearance from his IRA superiors to do so. They told him that they would rather he didn't make a statement but they didn't have a problem with it if he did. On his own head be it, they said to him, and he was instructed to be wary of the gardaí and their underhand methods. He was not to bring anyone who had not been mentioned already into the equation.

'A lot has been written about what my wife is supposed to have said to me – that she put pressure on me to to give a statement – but that is all untrue,' Heapes recalls. 'I love my wife and family and would never do anything to hurt them. Whatever I have done, I don't mind taking the rap for it, but my family should be left alone. As much as I love and respect my wife – and believe me, I would do whatever she asked me – she would never ask me to do something like give a statement or make any sort of ultimatum to me.'

Heapes spoke to Detective Garda Pat Mulcahy and gave a statement but refused to sign it. The statement read as follows:

I first met Catherine Nevin in the Sinn Féin advice centre in 1985. This is the Sinn Féin office in Finglas. I was introduced to her by members of Sinn Féin. She was a regular visitor to the centre and I met her frequently. I got an invitation for myself and my wife to attend the official opening of Jack White's Inn. Myself and my wife attended the opening and stayed for two nights. At the opening I was introduced to Willie McClean. He was at the time working there. I found out later that Willie McClean and Catherine were having an affair.

Some years after I first met Catherine Nevin, she approached me in Finglas one day and asked me to go for a drive with her. Catherine was at the time driving a large white-coloured car. She drove me to the Phoenix Park. She told me she was having trouble with her husband. I knew her husband, Tom Nevin, personally. She said that he was making her life hell. She said that he was beating her up and that he was having affairs. She also said that the money that had been used to buy Jack White's had been her money and that he gave her no money. I found that very hard to believe because I knew Tom and whenever I saw Catherine she always had plenty of gold jewellery and money and was often just after returning from holiday and was very well tanned.

She turned around and asked me would I get rid of Tom. She said she wanted him shot dead. I was kind of taken aback when she said it. I thought it was a wind-up. I said to her that costs money. She started about that on a bank holiday weekend he would be carrying between £20,000 and £25,000 cash. I said £25,000 is not worth a person's life. At this stage I was thinking this wasn't a wind-up and that this woman was serious. I said to her leave it with me and get back to me in a week or so. I went and told people of what I had been propositioned. These people thought it was a wind-up, but if she came back I was told to get as much detail off her and report back.

A few weeks after the first meeting she approached me again and brought me back to the Phoenix Park. She asked me did I think about what she asked me. I said that nobody would do it for that kind of money. She said, 'Well what are you talking about?' I said that there would have to be more money because there would have to be cars and motorbikes and guns bought and they would have to be untraceable. She said that there was a double insurance policy on Tom's life and that she would pay after it had been collected. I said to her that no one would do a murder unless they got the money up front. I told her to come back to me if she could come up with the money. I reported all this back to other people. They told me to keep in contact with her and report back to them.

About two or three weeks later, Catherine Nevin approached me again and we went back to the Phoenix Park, where she told me that she thought that she had resolved the problem about the money. She said that she reckoned that she could skim money off Jack White's each week and would open an account in her maiden name and not tell Tom. I said to her to get back to me when there was money in the account. Some four or five weeks later she approached me again and once more we went to the Phoenix Park. She took out from her purse a bank book with lodgements in it. I can't remember the amount or the name of the bank but she showed me a name on the book which she said was her maiden name. I can't remember what the name was. When she showed me the bank book I realised that Catherine Nevin was serious about having her husband killed. I asked her what was the best way to go about it. She asked her was I in a hurry and I said no.

She brought me up to a house off the South Circular Road. This house is in a row of terraced houses on the right-hand side of the road as you turn right off the South Circular Road when driving towards the Rialto entrance of James's Hospital. She stopped outside a house and said that this is Tom's first stop after he leaves Jack White's pub. He usually had a barman or handyman that worked in Jack White's with him. She said that the barman would go in and collect the rent from the two houses and he would give the money to Tom. She said that this would be a perfect place to do him. I said that the streets were too small and there were too many cars parked on them, we couldn't sit in a car and not get noticed. She said to me that she would arrange to get keys for the front door of the house and we would wait inside the hall for him as the apartments would all be empty as the people would all be at work by the time Tom arrived. With the narrow doorway, small garden with iron railings and gate, by the time we got past, your man Tom would be gone. I said to her that you better come up with a better idea. We left it at that and I reported back and they were taking it very seriously at this stage.

About three days after this meeting we met again. Catherine took me on a drive from their flats off the South Circular Road. We travelled from the South Circular Road into Islandbridge and into the Phoenix Park and as we were driving she told me that this was the route that Tom took and that he drove fast – at around 70 mph – all the time to make the bank before it closed for lunch and that if he missed the bank at lunchtime he would drive on to Clonee and he would park directly outside the window of the Grasshopper pub. He would leave the takings of Jack White's in the boot of the car with the alarm on and would watch the car while he was having lunch. When he was finished lunch he would head back towards Blanchardstown and stop at Kepak in Clonee to collect meat for the pub.

Catherine and I travelled the exact route from the flats to Clonee that Tom travelled every Monday or, in the case of a bank holiday weekend, on a Tuesday. While we were outside the Grasshopper pub in Clonee, Catherine said that this was the perfect place to do him. Then she drove me back to the Phoenix Park and brought me down a slip road near Wellington Monument. She stopped the car and she showed me the view of Islandbridge. From this point you could see the road at Islandbridge coming from the direction of the flats. She said that from this point we could see Tom's car crossing the bridge and follow it and that we could time his arrival there and his journey from there. We then discussed money. We had agreed £35,000. That was £10,000 up front and £25,000 in takings. I said, 'Leave it with me for a few weeks until I time Tom on his runs.' I reported back again from the impression I got then, knowing how serious the matter was that action would be taken to stop the matter, either by telling Tom or calling Catherine in.

But a couple of days later she arrived out in Finglas and brought me for a drive to the Grasshopper pub in Clonee. We parked on the opposite side from the pub. She said she was thinking over the last couple of days, that she thought she hadn't got a good alibi, and she said that if she was with Tom she would make sure that he would miss the bank for lunchtime and would have to go to the Grasshopper pub for lunch with the money. That would give her a perfect alibi by being with him. I said to her that it would be too dangerous for her. If someone was being shot there was no telling where the bullets might go. Catherine said, all the better: if she was wounded, that she would really look the part of the grieving widow.

I asked her how I was to get the money out of the boot of the car, could she get me a spare key. She said that Tom would have the keys in his hand coming out of the pub and to take it off him, as he wouldn't be able to do anything as he would be dead. Catherine also stated that she would make sure that Tom left the Grasshopper pub first. At this meeting Catherine said that the coming St Patrick's Day weekend would be the ideal time to do it. I said that it was too short notice as there was too much work to be done to set it up.

I asked her was she sure about the takings that it was the amount. Catherine said that on a bank holiday weekend the takings from the pub are left in the garda station in Wicklow each night over the weekend. I think it was Wicklow station she said. Tom would collect the takings there on the Tuesday morning on his way to Dublin. She said that there were two gardaí who kept the money for them in their lockers. I went back and reported the details of this meeting with Catherine and I was told not to worry, that something was being done straight away.

A few days later I heard that some people had gone out to Catherine at Jack White's or had brought her to Dublin and told her that they knew what she was up to and that it was over and if they heard that she was making an approach to anyone else to have Tom Nevin murdered, they would go and inform Tom and deal with her and whoever she got in contact with. That was the last I heard from Tom or Catherine Nevin for a couple of years.

Signing the statement was never an option for Heapes. The republican movement was in a state of flux at the time and it was possible that the decision to cooperate with the state against Catherine Nevin would be rescinded. Not signing gave him the option of denying at a later stage that he had made the statement, but if there were no objections he would be able to validate the statement at the deposition hearings the following year. This is in fact what he did.

To compensate for not signing, he offered the gardaí a guided tour of all the places he had gone to with Catherine Nevin where she had suggested her husband could be shot. With Detective Pat Mulcahy, Heapes retraced his and Catherine Nevin's movements, taking Mulcahy to Phoenix Park, South Circular Road and Clonee – all places on Tom Nevin's weekly route. As far as the investigating team was concerned, this was the second solicitation in the bag, even if they didn't have a signed statement.

3 August

Willie McClean was arrested under Section 30 of the Offences Against the State Act and taken to Crumlin Garda Station, where he was interviewed at length about his involvement with Catherine Nevin. Unlike Jones and Heapes, McClean had no problems telling his side of the story. The gardaí had hoped he would be able to shed some light on Catherine Nevin's habits and acquaintances and, given that McClean himself had substantial underworld contacts, the possibility that he might have been directly involved in the murder himself was raised.

McClean's statement was more concise and to the point than those of either Jones or Heapes. He did not talk much about his affair with Catherine Nevin but was more forthcoming about the solicitation:

I would say about 1990, myself and my present girlfriend were out for a drive and we decided to call into Jack White's for a jar. Catherine was there and spoke to us. She was chatty enough. That day I was driving DIL 5206, an Opel Kadett. I had parked the car outside the pub. We had about four or five jars and left. I didn't have any contact until about six to eight months later. She had asked me if I had a telephone number. I told her if she wanted to contact me she should ring the Irish House pub, in Harold's Cross. Catherine Nevin rang me at the Irish House pub. I can't remember exactly when. She rang me from St Vincent's Hospital, it was about evening time. She asked me to call out to the hospital to see her. She told me she was in hospital for some kind of heart complaint.

I called out to St Vincent's the next day. Catherine was in a private room. She was very chatty and friendly. She said she still loved me and wanted to start the affair again. It was a non-starter for me anyway. I told her I didn't want to go again. She went on a bit about getting back together. Suddenly she asked me to do something for her. She said, 'There is £20,000 there to get rid of Tom. You and I could get back together.' I was shocked and I said, 'Fuck off, Catherine. Where would this happen?' Catherine said, 'Get him going to the bank or at the flats.' She said, 'You would have the contacts.' I was shocked and said, 'No fucking way,' got up and walked out.

The fact that McClean professed openly and without equivocation that he had been solicited by Catherine Nevin to kill her husband and was prepared to testify to as much in court was the proverbial icing on the cake for the investigation team. Whether the two republicans would actually make depositions hung in the balance, and to have at least one solicitee ready to testify was a relief to the investigators, to say the least.

*

A remarkable set of negotiations then took place between the murder investigators and the IRA through an intermediary. These talks were held initially to secure the involvement of the republican witnesses in the State's case against Catherine Nevin and, secondly, because the investigators believed that the murder might have been committed by a renegade republican.

The first request to the IRA was made about two weeks after the Section 30s had been served. Detectives asked the IRA whether they could give them any more information on the murder; the message came back that the murderer was not a republican. A subsequent request – for help with the seemingly impossible task of locating the killer – was rebuffed too. The message back was that the gardaí already had statements from two republicans and that that was all they would be given. The third and last request was for more information as to whether the republican movement was aware of who was responsible for the murder. The message back was that the gardaí were looking in the wrong place if they were looking for the killer in the republican ranks. John Jones added a further proviso: if the harassment of anti-drug activists continued, he would be forced to withdraw his evidence.

A tacit agreement – although it was probably not sanctioned on the garda side – was made that the names of the two more important republicans, John Jones and Gerry Heapes, would be kept out of the papers. This constituted locking the gate after the horse had bolted, however: not long after their arrests, the two men's names had been leaked to the media.

Meanwhile, the IRA decided to conduct an inquiry of its own to determine just how involved with this Nevin woman the three republicans were. A republican source has confirmed that Russell, Heapes and Jones were hauled up in front of an IRA tribunal of sorts, but the three men in question have refused to comment on this. The men, I was told, were sent a message to meet a senior IRA figure at a rendezvous and, when they arrived, they were bundled into a van, had sacks placed over their heads and were taken to a secret location. They were then questioned for three hours before being bundled back into the van with sacks on their heads and dropped back at the rendezvous point.

By 4 November 1996, the gardaí had substantiated the statements made by the three principal witnesses and were ready to move onto the next stage: confronting Catherine Nevin with the new evidence. Detectives Fergus O'Brien and Joe Collins called into Jack White's; when they told her about the men's allegations, Catherine Nevin refused to speak and then handed them her solicitor's phone number on a piece of paper.

'Does this mean you do not want to comment?' Collins asked her.

'Yes, thank you very much. See my solicitor,' she replied.

It was January 1997 before Superintendent Pat Flynn, who was heading the investigation into the murder, decided that the gardaí had enough evidence to approach the Director of Public Prosecutions. At that stage, a lengthy file was sent; this file contained, among other things, details of eighteen main summary points.

Of these eighteen points, two refered to the solicitees: the first was that Catherine Nevin had solicited Heapes, Jones and McClean, and the second related to the erasing of Heapes's name and telephone number from Nevin's address book at some point between 12 and 18 April.

By April 1997 the Director of Public Prosecutions had given the green light to the indictment of Catherine Nevin on four counts: three of soliciting to murder and one of murder. She was subsequently arrested and charged with the murder of Tom Nevin at Ballinapark,

Arklow, on 19 March 1996.

The murder investigation still had a long way to go. Given the criminal records and criminal associations of the three principal witnesses and the uncertainty as to whether they would testify in court, a successful prosecution on the solicitation charges was not a foregone conclusion. The murder charge would be even harder to prove, as it in turn depended primarily on whether the solicitation charges were proved.

For Heapes, despite the occasional reminder of the case in the newspapers, Catherine Nevin was becoming a distant memory. He would face her again at the giving of depositions and during the trial itself but in between times he did his best to forget her. She hadn't forgotten him, however.

Word got back to Heapes that Catherine Nevin had been in Finglas with an unnamed gentleman looking for him. It appears she had tried most of the pubs and had talked to some of his friends but that no one gave her his address in Harristown Lane. Nonetheless, Heapes, suspecting garda involvement, was incensed. He expressed his anger to the gardaí when it came to the taking of depositions. They said that was the first they'd heard about the incident, and it was never reported in court.

Heapes believes that the fact that Catherine Nevin had gone looking for Heapes was being saved by the prosecution team for a new trial or an appeal – or in the event of their case going horribly wrong – because it proves beyond all reasonable doubt not only that Catherine Nevin knew Heapes but that she was trying to interfere with one of the witnesses in the trial. This was in direct contravention of her bail conditions. Nevin had spent four days in Mountjoy Prison after her arrest and had been released on her own surety of £5,000 and an independent surety of £20,000. Had this breach of bail conditions been reported, she would have lost her surety and her freedom and the case might have taken a very different course.

When the depositions were made later that year, it was the first time all three solicitees had been gathered together. It was also first time Jones and McClean had met. Indeed, despite the fact that Jones and Heapes were part of the same Sinn Féin *cumann,* they knew little about each other and led very different lives. Still, they were hardly in the mood to swap stories about Catherine Nevin. Given the choice, all three would rather have been somewhere else.

Jones, in particular, knew the pressure they would face on several fronts, The gardaí and the prosecution, Catherine Nevin's lawyers, the IRA and their own families would all be placing demands on them. The easiest thing for them to do would have been to walk away. But that was not an option. Jones felt that he had to tell the truth about Catherine Nevin and, if that seemed strange coming from a republican, he didn't care. Things had changed, and the old rule book did not cover something like this. He had to do what he thought was right.

The decision was taken by the prosecution team to put Jones into the witness box first at the taking of depositions, because it was felt that he was the most composed and would be able to show the others how to handle the situation. The opening exchanges were light-hearted but Jones knew that this was an attempt by the defence team to create a false sense of security before moving in for the kill. It was hardly surprising that, rather than question him on the more pressing matters of the case, Nevin's lawyers concentrated on the minutiae.

One of the defence lawyers noted that, when Catherine Nevin had first asked Jones to kill her husband, Tom, Jones had reported the incident to Patrick Russell and another senior republican. The lawyer asked Jones who this other republican was. Where he could have said, 'I don't remember', instead Jones tried to be honest. He said that he believed the other man was Noel Ellis – the father of Dessie Ellis – but could not swear to the court that he was sure of this. The result was a set-to with the defence as they badgered him in an attempt to rubbish his testimony. Then, rather then reiterating the fact that he could not remember who the person was, he changed tack and told the court that he was not in a *position* to tell them.

The defence could sense a breakthrough when Judge Mary Malone came in and saved him. 'You should give the name of the person you spoke to,' she told him.

Again Jones gave an ambiguous answer. 'Just a question to yourself. If I am not at liberty to give the name, that's the scenario I'm raising.'

But after the judge interjected again and said, 'You either know the name or you don't know the name,' Jones told the court he didn't know who it was.

Still, the defence could sense this was a weak point, and they were not about to let it pass. But they then slipped up themselves. The defence counsel, meaning to address Jones but forgetting his name, glanced at the list and asked Jones how he could forget this second man's name. The witness's response was, 'Yes, just as you have forgotten who I am.' The point was dropped.

Jones's experience in the witness box had not been lost on Heapes, who decided that he was not going to make the same mistakes. As with Jones, the defence team were interested in whom Heapes had reported Catherine Nevin's solicitations to, knowing that if they were senior republicans, Heapes would not be able to give their names and the defence lawyers could wear him down and discredit the rest of his testimony. But he was ready for them.

When they asked this question – as he knew they would – he told the court how he had told his mates 'Mickser', 'Redser' and 'Tommo' about Catherine Nevin in the pool hall and how they had all laughed at the prospect of Heapes being propositioned by her. Despite earnest appeals from the defence to the judge and vigorous cross-examination at the hands of the defence lawyers, Heapes's claims were accepted by the court. As he had not signed any statements, it was the deposition that would copper-fasten his involvement in the case. The prosecution breathed yet another sigh of relief.

Heapes made one significant correction to his statement: originally, he had not mentioned the very first occasion on which Catherine Nevin had raised the possibility with him of having her husband shot. He told the court she had approached him in the pool hall beside the Barry House and they had gone into the pub for a drink. After she had described to him a litany of abuses her husband was alleged to have perpetrated on her, she got to the point: would he kill her husband? Heapes claims he told her he would think about it.

McClean, while he did not have to contend with enquiries about superiors, had a bumpy ride at the depositions too. Various tactics were used by the defence to trip him up but he too was wise to their modus operandi and completed his testimony relatively unscathed.

If the three men had any doubts about how important they were to the case, these doubts were soon dispelled when they were told by the prosecution after the depositions that they *were* the case. It would be a little over two years before they would be gathered in court again, and this time it would be for real. A jury, the media, the hardest-hitting defence team in the land and the most sensational trial in Irish legal history lay ahead of them.

9

Court Diary

It would take almost four years before the case of the Director of Public Prosecutions versus Catherine Nevin would be heard. The size of the investigation – only the Veronica Guerin murder enquiry was larger – and a backlog of murder and rape cases rostered for the Central Criminal Court pushed the date for the trial into the new millennium.

The documentation for the investigation was condensed to a tenth of its original size of 2,000 pages and seven volumes for the DPP. It was envisioned at the outset that the case would probably last a month, given the number of witnesses due to be called, but the powers-that-be had reckoned without Catherine Nevin. The stage was set for one of the most fascinating court cases ever.

12 January: Day 1
The gathered throng in Court 2, with Mr Justice Carney presiding, heard Senior Counsel for the Prosecution Peter Charleton first tell the court that further discussion on some of the legal issues was needed before they could proceed with the case, and second request that Catherine Nevin be arraigned on the first count of murder only. Nevin was then asked how she pleaded:

'Guilty or not guilty.' She replied, 'Not guilty.' Mr Justice
Carney proceeded to swear in a jury of six women and
six men for the trial; these people were warned that
they would have to be prepared for a long haul.

The case was relocated to Court 3 and was allocated
Justice Mella Carroll as trial judge. The legal teams
that faced down each other in the court included, for
the prosecution, Senior Counsel Peter Charleton, a
Trinity law lecturer; the Chief State Solicitor's repres-
entative, Michael Kennedy; and Junior Counsel Tom
O'Connell; and for the defence, legendary Senior
Counsel and Queen's Counsel Patrick McEntee, Junior
Counsel Paul Burns and solicitor Garret Sheehan.

As with any murder case, there was a list of exhibits
contained in clear plastic bags. Exhibit No. 2 was the
scrap of paper bearing John Jones's phone numbers,
for work and home, and the number of another
prominent republican. In her testimony Catherine Nevin
denied that she had written the numbers and implied
instead that Tom had done so.

Exhibit No. 3 was another piece of paper found in
Catherine Nevin's bedroom, this time bearing three car
registrations, one of which – DIL 5206 – was that of a
car belonging to Willie McClean. Nevin said that it was
common practice to take down the details of suspicious
cars, though why she would take down the registration
of a car owned by the man with whom she was having
an affair at the time is not clear.

The fourth exhibit was Pat Russell's diary, which
records his meeting with Catherine Nevin in the
Davenport Hotel. The fifth was Nevin's own address
book, which bore the name and number of Gerry

Heapes scribbled out on its back and front covers. Exhibit No. 22 was the warrant authorising the search of Russell's offices in Merrion Square. The warrant, which had been issued under the Offences Against the State Act by Superintendent Jeremiah Flynn on 26 July 1996, also allowed gardaí to arrest and detain Russell for up to forty-eight hours. Exhibit No. 33 was a bank deposit book in the name of Catherine Scully, Catherine Nevin's maiden name. The book showed that Heapes's assertion that she had told him she had set up an account to siphon off funds to finance a murder was correct.

13 January: Day 2

Senior Counsel Patrick McEntee did not take long to get into his stride on the first day of the trial proper. In fact, he immediately tried to stop the trial before it had started in earnest by applying to have the charge of murder and the charges of soliciting to murder heard separately. He then attacked the media and told the court that his client had been so badly portrayed in the newspapers that she would not get a fair trial. He also argued that the gardaí were systematically leaking to the press matters relating to the case. The minds of jurors and potential replacement jurors would have been made up on the question of her guilt, he explained. In addition, the defence sought discovery of Special Branch files pertaining to Jones, McClean, Heapes and Russell. Then – for the first of many times – the jury was sent away while the opposing sides pursued the legal arguments.

Both McEntee's request for the separation of charges

and his appeal for a mistrial because of adverse media coverage were rejected but the argument over the Special Branch files would take longer to resolve. The problem was that, because Jones, Heapes and Russell were all republicans, their files were a matter of national security. Even though the IRA and Sinn Féin did not pose the same threat to national security that they once had, the Special Branch were very protective of their files and were loath to release them to the public. Miss Justice Carroll took the view that they would cross that bridge when they came to it.

McEntee's failed attempt to separate the charges was grounded in the belief – which was later proved to be correct – that the fate of the murder charge rested on the believability of the three principal witnesses and thus of the solicitation charges. The circumstantial evidence, although very strong, might not be enough on its own to bring a guilty verdict on the charge of murder. Given the colourful track records of the three principal witnesses, he was attempting to discredit their evidence and thus have his client freed.

14 January: Day 3
The behaviour of the press in their reporting of the case would become another recurring theme of the trial. Although the defence team's initial argument relating to the effect of media reporting on the jury was dismissed, Miss Justice Carroll told the jurors to be their 'own censors'. She rubbished the contention that the gardaí were deliberately leaking material to the press, however.

Nonetheless, although some of the broadsheets were

reporting the central legal arguments of the case, most of the tabloids were taking an even greater interest in the accused herself: what she was wearing, how her hair was styled and what colour her nails were painted. Catherine Nevin seemed to revel in – and even encourage – the notoriety she was gaining. The trial was fast becoming a media circus.

In court, Nevin was re-arraigned, and she pleaded not guilty to all four charges. She denied having solicited Jones, Heapes and McClean in 1989 and 1990 to kill Tom Nevin and also denied the murder of her husband in Jack White's Inn on the morning of 19 March 1996.

17 January: Day 4

Next, the matter of the Special Branch files had to be resolved. Never before had anyone sought Special Branch files for court proceedings. It is clear that the defence wanted as much ammunition as they could get to discredit the three principal witnesses; they were not sure what was in the files. In the end, Special Branch brought in its own lawyer, Senior Counsel Feichin McDonagh, who made every effort to distance his clients from the prosecution team.

The state, which was acting independently of the DPP, proposed that it would trawl the files and decide what information was important. This proposal was rejected out of hand by both the defence and the prosecution, however. Then, Miss Justice Carroll decided that the files should be made available to the prosecution and that they would decide what was relevant to the case and what was not.

18 January: Day 5

Counsel for the state told the court that the issue of the Special Branch files was under discussion. Attorney General Michael McDowell and the Garda Commissioner Pat Byrne, it seems, were trying to hammer out a solution to the impasse. They found themselves in a quandary, given that, on the one hand, there was a good chance that they would be taken to the Supreme Court and forced to hand the documents over if they refused access to the files, and on the other, they would be setting a dangerous precedent if they were to release the files. Appreciating the difficulty of their situation, Miss Justice Carroll allowed them some breathing space.

19 January: Day 6

Garda Commissioner Pat Byrne and the head of the Security Branch, Detective Chief Superintendent Jennings, attended the proceedings, and McDowell informed the Judge that the documents in question were held by Security Branch and not Special Branch and that they did not pertain to the case. He added that his clients would be seeking privilege on the grounds of lack of relevance and of national security.

Miss Justice Carroll was not impressed with the claim, wondering aloud why they would claim privilege if there was nothing relevant in the files. McDowell told her that they were motivated by the fear of setting a precedent with regard to the disclosure of Special Branch or Security Branch files.

20-21 January: Days 7-8

An accommodation was reached when it was decided that the files would be released to a senior official in the DPP's office, who would in turn advise Charleton and the prosecution of any relevant information that they contained. Miss Justice Carroll would then read the files if a problem arose. The defence objected to all but the last part of the arrangement, and for the rest of the case, where she thought it relevant, files were read by the judge herself. Needless to say, the jury were sent out of the courtroom during the legal argument over this issue.

24-25 January: Days 9-10

The jury had heard more than sixty prosecution witnesses over the first nine days of the case and, although Heapes, Jones and McClean had yet to give evidence, the case was already building up a head of steam. The focus of the prosecution case had initially been the murder itself and the finer points of the investigation at the murder scene, together with some lay testimony of the last few hours of Tom Nevin's life. But this all counted for nothing in the end.

26 January: Day 11

Patrick McEntee was in the middle of his cross-examination of Detective Sergeant Fergus O'Brien when a recess was called and everyone in the court filed out to go for lunch. When all the interested parties returned after lunch, it was clear that something was wrong. An hour and a half later, Justice Mella Carroll discharged the jury. It seems that one of the ushers in the court buildings had heard the deliberations of the jury from the balcony outside the jury room.

I have discovered that the three witnesses were told by the prosecution that the usher had overheard the jury say Nevin was guilty. Given that juries are not supposed to decide an accused's fate until all the evidence-giving and cross-examination is finished – and that the usher involved is from a parish quite near to Jack White's Inn – the judge's disquiet is understandable.

31 January: Day 12
After a four-day hiatus, the trial resumed and an attempt was made to select another jury. The case was transferred from Court 2 to Court 3.

1–4 February: Days 13–16
The defence team, led by McEntee, once more tried to stop the trial before it had even begun: they resubmitted an application about the portrayal of their client in the media. The consideration of this application would take up four days of argument. The upshot of these deliberations was that, on 2 February, Miss Justice Carroll took the unprecedented step of banning the press from either printing Catherine Nevin's photograph or commenting on her appearence.

The following day, seven journalists were put in the dock and were quizzed about their sources. The defence was alleging that gardaí had leaked to these journalists information regarding the more sensitive elements of the case. They refused to divulge these sources, however. Meanwhile, the judge for a second time dismissed the defence's contention that the gardaí were leaking information to the press.

7 February: Day 17
The second jury was sworn in but more legal debate delayed the start of the trial.

8-9 February : Days 18-19
After the second jury was discharged, it was revealed that one of the jurors was pregnant; she had told the judge that she might not be able to serve the time required on the jury. With only eleven jurors and at least a month of the trial ahead, the judge considered it too risky to proceed.

14 February: Day 20
A third jury was sworn in: after a stuttering start, the case was up and running again. Given the previous problems with jurors and the defence's delaying tactics, the new jury almost found themselves sequestered for the duration of the trial. As he had done with the first jury, Peter Charleton SC outlined the case, described what was expected of the jury and defined the charges that had been levelled against the accused.

The first witness for the prosecution was James Curry of Bell Communications, who recorded the time the alarm was activated on the night of the murder. Although this time did not tally with that given by Garda Sean Whelan, it hardly mattered because Garda (now Detective Garda) Paul Cummiskey had arrived a full fourteen minutes after the later of the times. Straightaway, this begged the question: what had Catherine Nevin been doing in the meantime?

15-25 February: Days 21-29

The focus for the prosecution in the first couple of days of evidence was to subject every claim made by Catherine Nevin to almost forensic examination. Piece by piece her evidence – what little she gave – was torn apart by each successive witness, and with each passing day her chances of being acquitted seemed to diminish. Still, it was one thing to prove she was a liar, and quite another to prove she had solicited someone to murder her husband.

28 February: Day 30

Jane Murphy, a former cleaner in Jack White's Inn, testified that she had taken phone calls for Catherine Nevin from John Ferguson, aka Pat Russell, and Judge Donncha Ó Buachalla. She also stated that she was not aware that Russell had visited the pub but was sure Ó Buachalla had.

28 February, the eleventh day of the trial and the thirtieth of court proceedings, would be one of the most significant because, when John Jones took the stand to give his testimony, he was creating history. Never before had a republican willingly given evidence in an Irish court.

And it almost didn't happen. Although the witnesses in a trial such as this are not supposed to talk to each other, Jones, Heapes and McClean had decided that enough was enough as far as their treatment by the media was concerned. Just before Jones was due to give evidence, the three got their legal representatives to approach the judge's bench to request a press ban because of the way they had been portrayed in the media.

'We had to endure the vilification of our names. We were labelled "Hitmen" and "Killers",' recalls Jones. 'The chief super told the judge that our very presence in court had cost us a great deal and we didn't deserve the sort of treatment we were getting. In the end the judge sided with us and banned Independent Newspapers and the *Irish Mirror* from printing photographs or reporting anything other than the court proceedings, and we were happy enough to proceed once that order was in place.' All three men are now seeking civil remedy for the injurious comments made about them by the media during the trial.

Jones's debut in the witness box was prefaced by the sworn testimony of Detective Garda Joe McKenna, who told the jury how he had first approached Jones. He testified that the initial exchanges were frosty, but Jones eventually agreed to talk.

After Jones had been called to the witness box, it was the prosecution's turn first, and Peter Charleton led Jones through his evidence. He was asked how he had first met Nevin and how she had managed to ingratiate herself with members of the Finglas *cumann* of Sinn Féin. Charleton then asked him a more direct question, one everyone wanted to hear the answer to: 'Did she have any involvement with your organisation herself?' To which Jones replied, 'None whatsoever.' He conceded, however, that she had allowed them the use of the pub for fund-raising events and to sell *An Phoblacht.*

Next, Charleton asked Jones about the soliciting; this was a crucial part of the prosecution case. Jones told the jury about Catherine Nevin's request and her persistence, and about how, in the end, he had had to tell her that it wasn't possible.

The only problem with Jones's testimony was his recollection of Catherine Nevin's black eyes – a point that he felt would clinch the case for the prosecution. Jones said that he had seen Nevin with black eyes some time in 1989 and 1990, but later, plastic surgeon Dr Michael Earley told the jury that Nevin had had an operation on her eyelids in September 1991 and that she would have had black eyes when she left hospital following the operation. This date fell outside Jones's time-frame.

If Jones had had it easy with Charleton, things were about to get much more difficult under Patrick McEntee's cross-examination. But Jones was ready for him.

29 February: Day 31

'I wanted McEntee to go for it, and for me it was all or nothing,' Jones recalls. 'Whatever had to come out, I didn't care, even if it made me look bad. I wasn't going to give him a licence to make a fool out of me. I had thought long and hard about a strategy and I had come up with three possible routes he might take. In the end he took the easiest of the three – the easiest for me, that is. Calling him by his first name was all part of my plan to show him that I didn't care what he said and, to be honest with you, I think it put him off. [McEntee acknowledged the following day that the exchange had been the most stressful in his forty years of legal practice.] He expects witnesses to be overawed and some of them are but I took every opportunity to mess with his head. At one stage he was babbling away in legalese and I just said to him, "Paddy, speak the Queen's English", which was a strange request from a republican. The problem was that McEntee had acted for me before and [Garret] Sheehan knew me too, so there was no telling what they'd come up with, but looking back I think I got off lightly.'

McEntee's first approach was to quiz Jones on his relationship with Dessie Ellis. Jones merely stated the obvious: firstly, that Ellis was a TV-repair man, and secondly, that he was involved with the IRA. This answer rendered the Defence Counsel's approach virtually useless. Then McEntee tried to trap Jones into confirming Catherine Nevin's contention that it was Tom and not her who harboured republican sympathies. When McEntee suggested that Tom had given them permission to sell *An Phoblacht* in the Barry House, however, Jones was clear that it was Catherine who had allowed them to do so. Jones was then asked to clarify Catherine Nevin's story about the two SAS men whom, she alleged, had attacked her in one of the flats on South Circular Road. 'I've never heard such a load of rubbish in my life,' Jones said.

Then the subject matter became more difficult. Why hadn't Jones reported Catherine Nevin to the gardaí, McEntee asked. Jones told the court that this was primarily because of the treatment he and his family had received at the hands of Special Branch. Why then hadn't he told someone in the IRA about her? Jones replied that he wouldn't have known how to contact members of the IRA. When the subject of Killinarden was broached, Jones denied all knowledge of it, and when, predictably, the subject of his only previous conviction was raised, he answered truthfully. He knew at that stage that McEntee was finished with him. During a break in Jones's evidence, the prosecution team asked him not to engage with McEntee but to direct his answers to the judge and jury. Jones obliged, but it was all over.

With his time in court over, Jones had just one more adversary to face: the media. On Jones's first day of giving evidence, Heapes and McClean had decided to face the press as they left the court, but Jones had made up his mind that he wasn't going to make things easy for them. All the newspapers and TV stations were desperate to get a picture of Jones, but so far no one had managed to. After Heapes and McClean left the court, they decided to approach Jones, who was having a coffee in the cafeteria at the Four Courts.

'I had tried several exits but each one was going to lead me out to where the gathered media were waiting,' Jones recalls. 'I could have put something over my head but I had done nothing wrong. No, I was going to outsmart them. I decided to have a coffee in the cafeteria when one of the TV cameramen sat down beside me and told me there was no escape and that I was going to have to face the music some time. He said that all they wanted was a fifteen-second segment of me walking out of the courts. I told him that I wasn't happy about the situation and about the possible repercussions for my family, but I told him I'd think about his request and I asked him to leave me to gather my thoughts. Then I saw my escape route. I imagine the kitchen gets very hot and I noticed they had one of the fire doors open. I asked the girl behind the counter where it led and she told me it led out beside the Bridewell. "You've had a hard day," she said to me, and she asked me did I want to leave out that door, and I told her I did but that I had to make sure there was no one waiting out the back. I went up to the rotunda, where all the TV people were gathered, and told them that I'd made up my mind: that I would do what they'd asked and that I'd be leaving in a few minutes. They said they were sorry to hassle me like that and said that it was only their job. With that, the word went out that I would be coming out the front exit in a few minutes, so they all gathered out there with their cameras set up, waiting for me. I went back to the cafeteria and straight out the door, across the green and into a taxi. I had escaped, and I'm sure they were sick.'

Jones knew the media weren't going to fall for the same bluff twice, so when he went into court the following day he had a contingency plan. The camera-men had appreciated his cunning but warned him that he wouldn't be able to pull the same stunt again. Nonetheless, the minute he stepped out of the witness box and Heapes became the centre of attention, Jones was ushered out of the fire door in the courtroom to a waiting car and was sipping on a drink in Jury's Hotel in Christchurch by the time the press realised he was gone.

Jones did his best to avoid eye contact with Nevin in the courtroom and maintains that he was totally unaware of her during Patrick McEntee's cross-examin-ation. Even today, however, he can barely contain his odium for the woman. 'I despise and resent what she tried to do to the republican movement,' he says. 'To even suggest that the IRA would carry out such an attack just so we could line our own pockets. I was prepared to do what no republican had done before to make sure she paid for her crimes.'

Gerry Heapes took the stand in the afternoon session of Jones's second day. Like Jones, Heapes was led through his evidence, this time by junior prosecution counsel Tom O'Connell. Heapes told the jury about his first meeting with Catherine Nevin and how he and his wife had received an invitation to the opening of Jack White's Inn. Then, incident by incident, he gave a full account of the way in which she had solicited him to murder her husband. He was candid about the fact that, years later, he had made an unsuccessful attempt to extort money from her.

1 March: Day 32

Heapes, like Jones, knew the worst was yet to come, but he too was prepared for an onslaught from Patrick McEntee. First, McEntee asked Heapes to outline his IRA background and involvement with Sinn Féin. When Heapes, again like Jones, was asked why he hadn't reported Catherine Nevin's proposals to him to the gardaí, he reminded the jury that he had never had a good relationship with Special Branch and the gardaí.

When Heapes went to visit his doctor a few days after his testimony, the doctor was able to offer him a diagnosis before he had even seen him. 'Selective amnesia' was his affliction, the doctor told him. In the witness box, Heapes could not remember the year the solicitations had taken place, but the fact that he could remember the type of car that Catherine Nevin was driving and that Tom Nevin had only had the car for a year made it easy to establish the time-frame for the events.

But McEntee wasn't going to let Heapes get away so easily when Heapes said he couldn't remember the real names of 'Redser', 'Mickser' and 'Tommo'. Nonetheless, as hard as he tried, the lawyer couldn't get Heapes to elaborate in this area In the end, a big smile broke across Heapes's face and the defence knew that the game was up.

2 *March: Day 33*

Willie McClean was the last – but by no means the least important – of the three principal witnesses to take the stand. After the prosecution had drawn from him the bones of his story, he was at the mercy of the defence – but not Patrick McEntee this time, who deferred to his junior, Paul Burns.

Burns grilled his charge with questions about his smuggling past and, when he felt he had extracted enough from McClean, he called him a liar who was 'in the business of peddling false pretences to obtain benefit for himself'. It mattered little what Burns thought of McClean, however, because the latter's evidence was soon corroborated by Sister Mary Baptist, who in 1990 had been chief executive of St Vincent's Hospital and who confirmed that Catherine Nevin had been admitted to the hospital twice in 1990. Nevin's first admission to the hospital was between 3 May and 11 May, to a four-bed ward, according to Sister Mary, and the second was between 25 October and 31

October, in a single room, just as Willie McClean had told the jury.

Unlike the other two solicitees, who did their best to ignore Catherine Nevin, Willie McClean made a point of staring at her. Even now, he can barely contain his anger towards her. 'If she had been a bloke, I would have busted her right there in the court and they could have taken me away and I wouldn't care,' he says. 'She lied through her teeth, denying our affair and saying she didn't know me. By God, I bet she knows me now.'

3–8 March: Days 34–37

Just before Jones, Heapes and McClean had given their evidence, the testimony of former cleaner Liz Hudson had caused a stir when she had suggested, in her evidence, that Catherine Nevin had conducted an affair with Judge Donncha Ó Buachalla. For the next four days, the focus of the case was on him.

9 March: Day 38

Witnesses in the Nevin trial were not allowed to compare notes about their testimonies, but as far as John Jones was concerned, once his fellow Sinn Féin member and friend Pat Russell had taken the stand, his own version of events would be corroborated and people would see Catherine Nevin for the cold-blooded killer that she was. He assumed too that Russell would follow the precedent that he had set and would be candid about republican matters in the witness box. Jones was in for a shock.

Of all the prosecution witnesses, Russell was perhaps the kindest to Catherine Nevin. He described their relationship as being a business one and explained that she had reactivated this relationship when she had approached him to do the pub's accounts. She had told him that she wanted to buy Tom's share of the pub and that Tom was drinking heavily. Russell had declined to do her accounts but had set her up with someone who would: Noel Murphy. Nevin had wanted him to keep their meetings secret and had given him an alias, John Ferguson.

As Russell had been so nice to his client, McEntee went easy on him in his cross-examination. It was at this stage that Jones and Russell's seventeen-year friendship came to an end.

The prosecution team were flabbergasted too, because Russell had pulled the ultimate fast one. A man with a great deal to lose – and with many questions to answer as to the real nature of his relationship with Catherine Nevin – had set the ball rolling for the investigation when he had given his first statement. Russell was forgiven for his earlier indiscretions but he still stood to lose everything if McEntee dug too deep. The witness's response was to seem almost complimentary to Catherine Nevin in his evidence, and then, as he correctly surmised, the defence would leave him alone. As a result, he emerged relatively unscathed from a trial that could have blown his world of murky deals wide open.

10–13 March: Day 39–40
Retired garda inspector Tom Kennedy took the stand to refute allegations that he had conducted an affair with Catherine Nevin. Although Kennedy had been

listed as a prosecution witness, Peter Charleton did not want to call him because he considered him of greater use to the defence.

Charleton attempted to strike a deal with the defence team whereby Kennedy would be given to them on condition that he would be cross-examined by the prosecution. Miss Justice Carroll would not allow this, however: and Tom Kennedy was going to be a prosecution witness, whether they liked it or not.

The prosecution case was closed; they had called 160 witnesses, some of whom had taken the stand twice in the trial and retrial. Now the big question was whether Catherine Nevin would take the stand. The rest of that day, a Friday, and the following Monday were taken up with legal argument, but by the afternoon of Tuesday 14 March, Catherine Nevin was ready and willing to take the stand.

14 March: Day 41

Catherine Nevin had been destroyed by the prosecution but she was not going to give up without a fight. Twenty minutes into her testimony, she dropped a bombshell that drew gasps from the gallery and groans from her legal team. She claimed that her husband, Tom, had been a member of the IRA.

After the case, Catherine Nevin would earn the moniker 'Black Widow'. Some commentators felt this was unfair, but everyone agreed that she could spin a complex web of deceit. Once in the box, she did her best to rubbish the testimony of virtually every prosecution witness.

Catherine Nevin claimed that Jones had been her

husband's friend and that she herself had never been in the Sinn Féin advice centre at 2A Church Street in Finglas. She claimed that her husband had been holding clandestine meetings with republican types and that she, being the dutiful wife, had not been party to what had been going on at these meetings. She alleged that Tom had first become involved in the republican movement in the early 1980s and that he had been spending so much time away from her that she had thought he was having an affair and had subsequently confronted him about this. If she had stretched the bounds of believability with her first claim, it was nothing compared with her second: that she had never strayed from her husband and that they had in fact enjoyed a healthy sexual relationship.

She then raised the issue of the proposed joint purchase of the Killinarden Inn by Tom Nevin and the IRA. Johnny Deery, a Northern republican, had supposedly taken £100,000 from the IRA's coffers and given it to John Jones, who was to be Tom Nevin's silent partner. Tom would put up the remaining £500,000 to complete the purchase. This deal, she said, had been copper-fastened at a meeting in the Green Isle Hotel which had been attended by herself – although she had earlier claimed she had not been party to her husband's alleged republican activities – Tom, John Jones, Johnny Deery and two Tallaght-based republicans, John Noonan and Dickie O'Neill.

She claimed that Tom had shown her a deposit book for an account containing £100,000 and that the deal had only fallen through because Jones and Tom Nevin had had a falling-out. According to Catherine Nevin, her husband and Jones had once been very close and, though she knew very little about the activities with which they were involved, she was aware, she told the court, that her husband had given Jones access to one of the flats the Nevins owned on South Circular Road.

Nevin then told the jury that she had been passing the flat late one night when she had seen a light on and had decided to go in. She alleged that, once inside, she had been assaulted by two men, who then promptly left the building. What she said next could have been an ingenious lie, but for the fact that she dressed it up with so much stupid detail.

When the men had gone out of the building, they had left behind them an assortment of wires and what Catherine Nevin described as 'components from the back of televisions', she told the jury. Jones had been a TV-repair man, and it had come to light in the trial of Jones's friend Dessie Ellis that the IRA was using circuit boards similar to those found in the backs of televisions. This ploy by Catherine Nevin could have added some veracity to her story, but she had neither the wit nor the wisdom to pull it off.

She denied that she had ever solicited Gerry Heapes to kill her husband or that she had conducted an extra-marital affair with Willie McClean, whom she claims she knew little about, apart from what her husband had told her. Again, she painted a picture of an ideal marriage between herself and Tom and vociferously denied that he had ever been violent towards her. She also rubbished allegations that she had cheated on her husband with retired inspector Tom Kennedy and Judge Donncha Ó Buachalla. She finished her testimony that day with more information about her husband and his republican activities.

15 March: Day 42

As the prosecution must disclose to the defence whatever evidence they will use, Patrick McEntee knew exactly what the prosecution witnesses were going to say and could structure his cross-examination accordingly. This was in stark contrast to the situation when it came to his own client. McEntee had no idea from one moment to the next what Catherine Nevin was going to say. Indeed, if anything, the prosecution had a better idea of what she was capable of. They had calculated that she would insist on taking the stand, would spout lie after lie and would end up contradicting herself. In the end, she had become the prosecution's most valuable witness.

Catherine Nevin's testimony on this day of the trial focused primarily on the night and morning of the murder, but she gave no satisfactory answers or explanations for her actions that night and only incriminated herself further. She must have realised that her freedom was slipping away from her and decided to have one last throw of the dice. The trial was about to descend into farce.

16 March: Day 43

Peter Charleton had waited a considerable length of time to get the chance to cross-examine Catherine Nevin. If he had thought that this was going to be the day when he would get his opportunity, however, he would have to wait a little longer because, when the court convened at eleven o'clock, there was no sign of her.

It had been reported on the radio that she had collapsed at her flat on Mountshannon Road and had been taken by ambulance to the nearby St James's Hospital. The defence team were at a loss: they were as flummoxed about what was going on as everyone else. The jury were sent away without explanation, which left the prosecution, and especially Peter Charleton, in no doubt that the incident was a tactic to engender sympathy for the accused.

Dr David Green of St James's Hospital took the stand in the afternoon to enlighten the court as to the exact nature of Catherine Nevin's ailments. He told Miss Justice Carroll that the toxicology report on her blood had revealed that she had ingested three drugs: the sedative Dalmaine, the painkiller Tylex and the diuretic Spironolactone. Although he could not establish when the pills had been taken, he could tell the court that Catherine Nevin would be ready to take her place in the witness box again by Wednesday.

22-27 March: Days 44-47

When the court reconvened after another enforced break, a tired and no doubt angry Judge Carroll demanded an explanation from Catherine Nevin. The accused claimed that she had returned home on the evening of 16 March to find her flat open and an intruder, whom she had inadvertently tripped over. The man, who had been wearing an anorak, was, she claimed, an old republican friend of her husband's, although she could not remember his name.

Nevin said that she had been told by this man that

she had been naming people in court that she shouldn't name; he had then warned her not to name any more, she said. Then, she alleged, he forced her to swallow some pills and the next she knew, she was in hospital.

Before the prosecution could begin their cross-examination, Nevin made some final contributions: that Tom had been an alcoholic and that she had never told carpet-fitter Donnchadh Long that she planned to kill her husband. She finished by denying that she had ever solicited Gerry Heapes, John Jones or Willie McClean to kill her husband.

Peter Charleton might have been forgiven for taking an aggressive approach with the accused under cross-examination, but he prefered to let the accused inflict damage on herself. Time after time, she obliged. When he finally tired of her ramblings, he accused her of 'spinning a gigantic yarn', but she maintained that she was in court 'to tell the truth'. Charleton attacked her too over what he perceived to be a 'gross defamation and character assassination' of her husband.

She then issued point-blank denials of having had affairs with former garda inspector Tom Kennedy and Judge Donncha Ó Buachalla and attributed any IRA involvement relating to the events surrounding her husband's death to Tom Nevin, who of course was not there to defend himself.

28 March: Day 48

One of the most heartening aspects of the trial was that Tom Nevin's family were given a chance to rebut Catherine Nevin's outrageous claims. Local gardaí concurred with the family's portrayal of Tom as a warm, law-abiding and certainly not subversive Galway-man who had the misfortune to become involved with the wrong woman.

The Nevin family's reaction to the three men who had been asked to kill their relative was typically gracious. Patsy Nevin had shaken each man by the hand at the taking of depositions and had thanked them. 'It made me feel like I was doing the right thing when Patsy shook my hand,' John Jones remembers. 'He asked me did I know who killed Tom and I told him I didn't but I hope they find whoever did it. After my first day of evidence at the trial, some relative or friend of the Nevin family approached me and asked me was I John Jones and I told him I was but that I didn't know who he was. "I'm from Galway and I want to thank you for what you're doing and it's been a pleasure meeting you," he said, and that put me at ease because we really didn't know how the Nevin family would see us, especially in view of the fact that we had known that Catherine planned to kill her husband and we hadn't told the guards.'

29 March: Day 49

In his closing speech, Tom O'Connell, junior counsel for the prosecution, asked the jury to consider the testimony of Catherine Nevin in relation to the evidence given by the twenty-four main prosecution witnesses. Who was lying: Catherine Nevin or the twenty-four, who inluded an assistant garda commissioner?

O'Connell told the jury that the prosecution had exposed 'two enormous lies': the first, her allegation that Tom Nevin had been a member of the IRA, and

166

the second, her denial that she had had affairs with Kennedy and McClean, amongst others. How then, the junior counsel asked, could any of her evidence be believed?

30 March–7 April: Days 50–56
In his summing-up of the defence's case, Patrick McEntee delivered a gargantuan speech: it lasted ten hours and spanned four days of court proceedings. In the course of this speech, he did a great deal to redress the balance a little in favour of the accused.

McEntee asked the jury to consider some fundamental questions. To begin with, could they in all honesty, he asked them, rely upon the evidence of Gerry Heapes, John Jones and Willie McClean? In his closing comments, the lawyer described Heapes as a 'liar', called McClean 'a conman who lives by his wits' and said there was 'a big question mark' over Jones. Finally, he asked the members of the jury whether they would 'buy a second-hand motor car off any of them'. But had McEntee done enough to negate the contributions made by the three witnesses?

The defence counsel had also tried to bolster his client's claims by saying that the reason that Catherine Nevin had not told the gardaí about her husband's involvement with the IRA was because she feared the possible repercussions of such a move. In the end, though, this was all too little too late for the accused.

Whatever advances the defence had made in the summing-up over their prosecution counterparts were soon rendered useless when it was the turn of Miss Justice Carroll to deliver her directions to the jury.

The judge made no apologies for the backgrounds of the three men and noted that the prosecution had given the jury a warts-and-all portrayal of Heapes, Jones and McClean. The jurors were to accept them for who they were; they did not have to believe everything they had been told in evidence but could rather pick and choose, discarding anything that did not relate to Catherine Nevin.

Miss Justice Carroll also instructed the jury that there was a great deal of 'similar fact' evidence in the contributions of Heapes and Jones but that, with McClean, because there was no mention of staging Tom's murder after a bank holiday weekend and making it look like a botched robbery, there was very little that was similar. Nonetheless, McClean's testimony was probably just as important as the others, the judge said, because it provided a motive: collecting the proceeds of Tom's insurance policies. The judge also fired a broadside at the defence team for the character assasination they had performed on the deceased and she had consulted the relevant Security Branch files to confirm that the allegations that had been made were false.

To the detached observer, it seemed an open-and-shut case, and many commentators were predicting a quick guilty verdict from the jury on at least three of the four counts. I spoke to one garda superintendent who thought differently: he told me, the day the jury began deliberating, that he found that juries were becoming increasingly conscientious and that, in view of the volume of evidence the jurors had to consider, he would not be surprised if no verdict had been reached by the start of the following week. This man was to be proved right.

8-11 April: Day 57-60
The country held its breath when the jury retired. Although people expected the jurors to return with a verdict quickly, this did not happen; it became patently clear at an early juncture that the jury were taking their brief seriously. From time to time, a representative would leave the jury room to ask advice from the judge on a point of law.

John Jones was a concerned man when, late on Saturday evening, the jury asked for direction on his evidence. The query pertained to the story of the Catherine Nevin's black eyes and the fact that the recorded date of her eyelid operation fell outside the timescale that Jones had given for the solicitations. Miss Justice Carroll directed the jury that the time-frame Jones had given could not be extended to incorporate 1991.

On Sunday evening, when it was clear that a unanimous verdict would not be acheived, the judge told the jury that she would accept a majority verdict. At that stage, many observers thought that a decision from the jurors was imminent, but a verdict was not forthcoming. Monday passed, and there was still no decision. In fact, it wasn't until Tuesday, when the jurors had been sequestered for a record four nights (in the K Club) that they finally arrived at a verdict.

It was 6.40 pm on Tuesday 11 April when the verdict was delivered. When the news filtered through, Willie McClean was exactly where he had been the day

Catherine Nevin had asked him out to St Vincents's Hospital: in the Irish House. John Jones was at home in Balbriggan, waiting patiently by the phone and Gerry Heapes was in the recovery ward of Bon Secours Private Hospital after a routine operation. The exchange in court was as follows:

'On Count 2 [soliciting John Jones]. You say the accused is guilty on Count 2?'

'Yes.'

'Was that the verdict of all of you?'

'The verdict of eleven of us. One dissented.'

'On Count 3 [soliciting Gerry Heapes]. You say Catherine Nevin, the accused, is guilty on Count 3?'

'Yes – the verdict of us all.'

'On Count 4 [soliciting Willie McClean]. You say the accused is guilty on Count 4?'

'Yes.'

In the excitement, the jury were not asked how many of them had agreed with the decision. In fact, it had been a majority verdict of 11 to 1.

'On Count 1[the murder of Tom Nevin]. You say Catherine Nevin is Guilty on Count 1?'

'Guilty, yes. That is the verdict of us all.'

In passing sentence, Justice Mella Carroll told Catherine Nevin that she had had her husband assassinated and had then tried to have his character assassinated.

Outside, pandemonium was breaking loose as newspapers who had been prevented from commenting on Catherine Nevin oiled their printing presses and acres of column space were devoted to the trial. Some of the comment was downright vicious, and some of it was deserved. Even now, there is a great public interest in Catherine Nevin. The latest fad, especially among the tabloids, is to run Nevin's picture alongside any story relating to the women's section of Mountjoy Prison, regardless of whether she has anything to do with the story.

Heapes, Jones and McClean found themselves under siege too as wave after wave of photographers, cameramen, journalists and scriptwriters peppered them with phone calls and house calls. TV3 ran a documentary on Catherine Nevin and got their highest viewing figures ever; this film was made without the cooperation of the three principal witnesses.

At the beginning of the summer, two books, *The Black Widow,* written by Niamh O'Connor of *Ireland on Sunday* and published by O'Brien Press, and *The People Versus Catherine Nevin,* written by Liz Walsh of Magill magazine and published by Gill & Macmillan, fed the public's fascination with Catherine Nevin. It seems, however, that this appetite for information and gossip about Nevin has still not been sated.

7 June: Sentencing

Justice Mella Carroll could have lectured Catherine Nevin all day but probably figured that she would be wasting her time by doing so. Instead she proceeded without any fuss to the matter at hand – the sentencing. She sentenced Nevin to seven years on each of the three counts of soliciting, having already handed down the mandatory life sentence for murder.

Nevin's lawyers, Senior Counsel Patrick McEntee and Garret Sheehan, immediately sought leave to appeal her sentence, on more than twenty seperate grounds, and revealed that Jack White's Inn had been under investigation by the Garda Anti-Racketeering Unit on suspicion of having laundered IRA money but had later been struck off the list of the agency's targets. Miss Justice Carroll refused leave to appeal: Catherine Nevin would have to get used to an extended term in Mountjoy Women's Prison – her home for the forseeable future.

But the Nevin story was far from over. Liz Walsh of *Magill* had revealed, in an article in *Magill* which hit the news-stands within hours of the guilty verdict, that there had been some irregularities in the manner in which Catherine Nevin had been issued with a renewal of the pub license for Jack White's; at the time, she had been a suspect in the murder of the other co-licensee.

Judge Donncha Ó Buachalla had issued the licence to someone who was, at the very least, a close friend of his, and this called into question his impartiality, if not his judgement. The manner in which the licence was issued is under investigation in a public enquiry, chaired by Judge Frank Murphy, that is ongoing.

The guilty verdict provided closure for Gardaí Vincent Whelan and Michael Murphy, who were formally cleared of all charges laid against them and were fully reinstated. Judge Ó Buachalla is having to answer questions about his conduct towards the two guards. For instance, on 3 November 1995 in Arklow district court, Ó Buachalla had instructed that the two gardaí swear an oath before each case rather than just once, as was the normal practice, and had dismissed twenty-two of the twenty-six cases that the two men had brought before him. Meanwhile, Detective Garda Jim McCawl is suing Catherine Nevin for defamation of character, and the three principal witnesses, Gerry Heapes, John Jones and Willie McClean, are suing several newspapers for the same reason. If the case involving McCawl comes to court, it is bound to create a media frenzy because Catherine Nevin would give evidence at the trial.

Although a great deal about Catherine Nevin, her affairs and her murky dealings remains unknown, the most important fact is that the gardaí have still not found Tom Nevin's killer, nor does it seem likely that they will do so. The one person who has that piece of information is Catherine Nevin herself and, with the powers of temporary release available to the prison, she will be aware that some cooperation by her with the authorities might shorten her sentence.

The true nature of Catherine Nevin's relationship with the IRA has, it is now believed, been brought to light, but if she was playing each side against the other, exactly what was her relationship with the gardaí, and in particular the Special Branch? Did she contact them or did they contact her? Was she given any assignments? Had she ever been bugged? What information did she pass on to them about the activities of Sinn Féin and the IRA? Was this the real reason Special Branch or the Security Branch, or both, were so reluctant to hand over the files? Had Special Branch sent her to meet Jones in the first place to get to know him? Given the secretive nature of Special Branch, these questions will probably never be answered.

This case, which has made such a major impact, is not yet closed. Who was Tom Nevin's killer? If one were to profile the killer from the evidence given, the following conclusions could be drawn:

1   The killer was known to Tom Nevin. The manner in which Tom was found on the morning of the murder suggested that, whoever the killer was, he had not alarmed the victim unduly before the fatal shot.

2   The killer was desperate for money. He or she had to have been in order to undertake such a high-risk job for a relatively low return.

3   The killer was a skilled amateur but not a professional hit man. His or her choice of weapon – a shotgun with pellets normally used for deer-hunting – demonstrates this.

4   Tom Nevin did not feel threatened by his would-be killer. Tom was counting money at the time and, had he felt threatened, he would have taken evasive action to protect himself and the takings.

5   The killer was smart enough not to leave any clues. Whoever the killer was left no fingerprints or leads for the murder investigators to follow.

6   The killer was doing it for money and not for Catherine Nevin. This can be seen by the fact that Catherine Nevin had been persuaded to stage the robbery at Jack White's, where all her movements were scrutinised by staff and where she had to arrange the pub to look as though there had been a botched robbery.

7   The killer had obviously dismissed Catherine's

plans to have Tom shot in Dublin, possibly because that was too near – or maybe too far from – his or her home.

8   The killer took the job at short notice. If reports of Tom being followed have any truth in them, then a robbery en route had been considered and a snap decision to stage it in Jack White's had been taken. The fact that Jack White's was in a remote location and that gunshots would not be heard by anyone apart from those in the pub was probably the deciding factor.

9   The killer has disappeared from view. Better than saying nothing to the guards in an interview is not being in the country at all when they call around.

10 If Tom Nevin knew his killer, then the killer lived or worked in either Finglas, Dolphin's Barn or the environs of Jack White's. Tom spent a great deal of time in his own pubs and rarely socialised in other bars.

11 The killer left Tom's car by the canal off Leeson Street, close to Dolphin's Barn. This spot is also, however, just off the main route to Jack White's; the car could therefore have been left by someone who did not know the city.

12 The killer had no regard for human life and had probably served time in prison or a mental institution, or both. The murder of Tom Nevin, who had done little wrong to anyone, was cold-blooded.

13 No professional hitman would have taken on a job of this nature. With no evidence of a cash-up-front payment and a take for St Patrick's weekend which was well below what Catherine Nevin had suggested

to Gerry Heapes, the amount of money was not the prime motivation for the crime. In other words, the killer was desperate for any money he could get.

14 If the murder had been carried out by a band of renegade republicans, there is no doubt they would have taken some sort of revenge for the reduced payment for the hit – and would have had ample opportunity to do so.

15 The killer was not alone. Unless the killer lived locally, he or she must have been transported to the murder scene in a car other than Tom Nevin's Vectra. While the killer drove Tom's car to Dublin, somone else had to drive the first car home too.

16 The killer was familiar with the layout of the pub. Therefore this person was either a regular in the pub or had been in and out of it on the week of the murder. It is possible that Catherine Nevin had shown the killer around in the half-hour that Tom was away leaving one of the regulars home, but this seems unlikely.

17 The killer and his or her accomplice had arrived at the scene at least an hour before the murder. They could not have predicted accurately when the last drinker, a guard, would leave. In addition, if they arrived too late, Tom would have had the takings counted and they would not have been able to stage a botched robbery.

18 The killer and his or her accomplice spent that last hour inside the pub. Outside was too risky because Jack White's was beside the main road and the chances that a patrol car would pass by were fairly high. Most of the local gardaí would have been

familiar with the Nevins' routine, and any deviation from that routine would have aroused suspicion.

19 The killer is probably content in the knowledge that he or she will never be caught. Even if Catherine Nevin points the finger, who would believe her? There is no corroborating evidence. Catherine Nevin would have to present investigators with something other than her word, which has no value now. It doesn't help matters that she has already given investigators a list of possible suspects as long as her arm and that she has a penchant for inventing ficticious characters.

20 The killer is still at large. As long as this is the case, Tom's brothers and sisters will not achieve any closure.

10

Who Is Catherine Nevin?

Catherine Nevin is an extremely mysterious figure. Both seasoned commentators and scholars have tried to fathom what she is all about but the best they can proffer is an educated guess. Only one person knows what goes on inside her head and that is Catherine Nevin herself. Meanwhile, working her out has become a national pastime and theories abound regarding what motivates her.

It is clear from the outset that Nevin was greedy and manipulative and that, although she coveted material goods, she desired power most of all. But where did this lust for power and greed for money originate? People who knew her before she moved from Nurney to Dublin find it virtually impossible to link her actions in recent years with the well-behaved and ambitious schoolgirl they knew in the 1950s and 1960s.

What happened that made her so cold and heartless? Had the seeds of hate and bitterness always been there but came to fruition only when she moved to the big city, or was the change in her the result of some catastrophic event? Again, only Catherine Nevin knows the answers to these questions.

Catherine Nevin's tenure at the Castle Hotel on Gardiner Row on Dublin's north side seems to have been a pivotal period in her life. In the early 1970s it was the most popular republican haunt in the capital, and it seems that working in the place at that time had a profound effect on the young Catherine Scully, as she was then.

During those years she forged friendships with many prominent republicans, not least Cathal Goulding, who had become the IRA's Chief of Staff in 1962 and who led the Official IRA after that organisation's split with the Provisional IRA in 1969. Their friendship seems to have endured for the better part of three decades, but it is unclear whether all that has changed in the wake of the trial.

Whether Goulding was aware that Catherine Nevin was courting the Provisionals at the same time is not clear but, given that the Castle Hotel, after the split, became the preserve of the Provisional faction, it is hardly surprising that this was taking place. Maybe he encouraged it and maybe Catherine Nevin got her first taste of subterfuge in this way – and liked it.

It seems entirely possible that Catherine Nevin had sexual relations with one or more of the patrons of the hotel and realised the power and control she could exert over men, regardless of their rank or standing. But then, a person's position in life was of the utmost importance to Catherine Nevin; she had no time for the rank and file.

Nevertheless, the environment in which she was working and the people she consorted with made her feel secure and empowered her. As the IRA have wielded so much power over the criminal underworld, volunteers have had a growing number of problems with family members and friends who think that, by name-dropping, they can manage any dangerous situation. Catherine Nevin was a serial name-dropper, and the prospect of IRA involvement was explicit in most of her threats.

Marrying Tom was a means to an end for her. If there had been any love in the relationship between the two of them, it disappeared when she, as Willie McClean alleges, had herself sterilised. Was she ridding herself of any possible heir or was it just a precaution she took while conducting her extramarital affairs?

Catherine Nevin's experience in the Castle Hotel seems to have been so memorable that she tried to recreate that atmosphere in the Barry House, another republican haunt but this time with a working-class clientele. Again she gravitated towards the people she perceived to be in positions of power. The trappings of republicanism were very much in evidence in the pub, at her instigation. When she and her husband moved to Jack White's, she tried to establish the same sort of republican contacts there, but by and large failed to do so.

Somewhere along the line, she had become involved with Special Branch. Whether they had been observing her consorting with republicans and had enlisted her or whether she made the approach and offered them information, we may never know, but there is a good chance that she was working for them before she moved to Finglas. This might explain her strange first meeting with John Jones and the fact that, despite her attendance at various rallies, she remained untouched by the Branch.

It was widely believed that the TV-repair shop in Church Street in Finglas which doubled up as the Sinn Féin advice centre was probably a bomb-making enterprise, yet successive raids on the place had yielded nothing. Special Branch needed someone who could get inside to see what was going on. Was Catherine Nevin that person?

She had proposed to Jones that an IRA arms bunker could be housed in the cellar of the Barry House – and, later, in Jack White's – and had also offered her services as a courier for the IRA. She had even given the IRA the use of one of the flats she and Tom had on South Circular Road as a 'safe house'. Was she setting a trap?

The members of Sinn Féin and the IRA who came in contact with Catherine Nevin would like to give the impression that they had her number straight away, but that is certainly not the case. In fact, I have discovered that at least one person left the Finglas *cumann* of Sinn Féin because of their discomfort with the amount of contact with the republican movement Catherine Nevin was being given.

It is interesting to note that the Barry House, while the Nevins owned it, and Jack White's had featured on a list of pubs under investigation by the Garda Anti-Racketeering Unit but were later removed from that list. Did that unit know about Special Branch involvement with Catherine Nevin or were they told about it at a later stage? Would this explain the reluctance of Special Branch or the Security Branch to bring their files on Catherine Nevin to court? They argued that they did not want to set a precedent, and surely if there had been anything remotely applicable to the case in the files, Justice Mella Carroll would have raised the matter. Now, however, we may never know the truth.

Still, the republican movement eventually found out about Catherine Nevin's Special Branch connections, and they kept her at arm's length from then on. When she solicited John Jones and Gerry Heapes to kill her husband, the feeling was that this was another ruse to trap republicans. The republicans failed to realise what we now know – that she was serious.

By the time she solicited the three men to kill her husband between 1989 and 1991, Catherine Nevin had climbed the social ladder as far as she would ever go. She was co-owner of a pub and some properties in Dublin and still she felt aggrieved. As far as she was concerned, these acquisitions were the product of her hard work, yet Tom would always be regarded as the owner of the pub and she would be seen merely as his wife. Not until she was the sole owner of Jack White's would she be taken seriously, she felt. That meant getting rid of Tom.

Outwardly, she made no secret of the fact that she wanted to get rid of Tom, but this related more to buying him out. If her step-aunt Patricia Flood is to be believed, privately, this wasn't an option for her. She wasn't going to let him leave, because that would reflect badly on her. If he had been murdered, then that was a different scenario altogether. In the first place, it cleared the way for her to become the sole owner of the pub, at no cost to herself. Even better, Tom's death would garner sympathy for her as the widow.

The solicitations at the beginning of the 1990s had

been terminated abruptly when the IRA had warned Catherine Nevin that she was not to solicit anyone else and that, if she did so, she would be forced to face the consequences and whoever she approached would be in deep trouble too.

She would heed the warning to begin with but she obviously saw fit to ignore it at some later stage. Another person who knew of the solicitations and the warning and yet maintained contact with Catherine Nevin up to the time of Tom's murder was Patrick Russell, aka John Ferguson. The republican movement, of which he was once an integral part, is still very angry about Russell's relationship with Catherine Nevin and has recently washed its hands of him.

Russell was the number one suspect in the murder of Tom Nevin for at least the first two – and possibly the first four – months of the investigation. Although he eventually cleared his name, he still has many questions to answer. He has portrayed himself as a legitimate businessman but there is very little that is legitimate about the way he conducts his business affairs.

Catherine Nevin's liaison with former garda inspector Tom Kennedy was a means to an end. In 1991 Catherine Nevin named Kennedy as her next of kin when a patient in hospital, and he might have thought that she genuinely cared for him. If her plan to take incriminating photographs of Kennedy in a compromising position in the flat on South Circular Road for the benefit of the IRA is anything to go by, however, she didn't think too much of him.

Judge Donncha Ó Buachalla is currently being

dragged over the coals by the enquiry into the nature of his relationship with Catherine Nevin. Leaving to one side the issue of the licence for Jack White's and his behaviour towards certain gardaí attached to Arklow Garda Station, there is some confusion as to exactly when he first met her. Ó Buachalla's version of events is that he became a regular visitor to Jack White's and became friendly with both Tom and Catherine Nevin shortly after he was posted to Arklow. But then, John Jones says Catherine Nevin had been raving about a hotshot solicitor called Donncha Ó Buachalla before his elevation to the bench.

The murder itself was as callous as it was gruesome, and the fact that Catherine Nevin had the composure to put on an act – albeit a bad one – after her husband had been shot dead says a great deal about her mindset. That she maintained that act throughout the investigation and then the trial, when she was in the public spotlight day after day, says as much about her mental strength as it does about her complete lack of scruples.

Some commentators have suggested that Catherine Nevin has all the signs of being a sociopath, but there is also an element of Munchausen's syndrome by proxy in her behaviour. Someone with this syndrome will willingly hurt a loved one in order to get public sympathy and notoriety.

There is no doubt that Catherine Nevin was in her element during the court proceedings. She courted the media and gave them plenty to write about every day, before Miss Justice Carroll put a stop to it. She was aware that people were watching her every move. Her clothes, nails and hair were groomed every day just enough to start tongues wagging, and even the books she read were supposed to tell the public something of her state of mind.

What is unique about Catherine Nevin's involvement in her husband's murder is that the solicitations were not motivated by a desire to escape a life of domestic abuse, nor were they the act of a woman jealous about her husband's affairs. Her involvement in the murder was motivated by greed and mabye even a little bloodlust. It is this that has captured the imagination of the public, who have never seen or read about anybody quite like Catherine Nevin.

We know from the testimonies of Gerry Heapes, John Jones and Willie McClean that Nevin had been planning the murder of her husband for almost a decade. Despite what they may think of her now, they were impressed at the time at the amount of thought she had put into these plans – so much so, that they were convinced that she was merely a mouthpiece for one or other garda agency.

There was still a large degree of naivety in her scheming, however, as was demonstrated at the murder itself. To stage the murder at Jack White's was a logistical nightmare for Catherine Nevin, and she soon realised that she was not as smart as she had thought she was. This was not the case for the killers, who have disappeared without a trace, leaving Catherine Nevin to carry the can.

Now and at least for the forseeable future, Catherine Nevin will be out of the public eye. It is not clear how she will deal with the harsh reality of prison. Both before and during the trial, there was compelling evidence that she spent most of her life in a world that she had created herself; now she will have to create an antidote to the enclosed surroundings of Mountjoy Women's Prison. She has at least seven years to think about it.

11

Tom Nevin – Rest in Peace

Amid all the brouhaha about Catherine Nevin, the judge, the IRA and the gardaí, the most important person in the equation has been forgotten: the murder victim. This author, however, along with many other people, has not forgotten Tom Nevin.

Tom Nevin touched a great many people with his kindness and sense of fairness. The pub could be said to be the urban farm, and for Tom, a Galwayman who had left a farm behind him, it was the next best thing. In a matter of years he had built himself up from barman to licensee but his demeanour never changed. He was a good landlord who valued his staff and treated them with respect and it seems he had a good head for business too. He was a very hard-working man who asked nothing of his staff that he wouldn't do himself and inspired loyalty from them as a result. Jack White's was a difficult place in which to work, and Tom brought grievances from cowering staff members to his angry wife.

With the information this author has gathered on Tom Nevin, it would be remiss not to set the truth about him in the public domain. Catherine Nevin did not just organise the murder of her husband, she sullied his name in court and, unfortunately, some of the mud has stuck. Clearing Tom Nevin of any criminal or subversive involvement might be the most important contribution this book has to make.

What was most impressive about the three men who were solicited to murder Tom was that their odium for Catherine Nevin was outweighed by both their desire to see that the architect of Tom's demise be brought to justice and the guilt they felt over his death. 'I regret not doing something more to stop her,' John Jones says, 'but I suppose it is easy in retrospect to say that. It was a very intense time and decisions were made to pursue a particular course. We had found out that Catherine was working for the guards and that was enough for us at the time. We just didn't want to get involved with her in any way, shape or form.

I wish things had been different, but when you gather all the information on her that we had, it leads you down a particular avenue. We just hadn't considered that she might actually go through with it. When I heard about Tom's death, I felt sick to the stomach, but who would have believed me if I'd told them? I regret not going to the guards straightaway after the murder with what I knew but I was acting on what I believed to be good advice from someone who I had thought was a friend, but now it seems he was acting in his own selfish interests.

Let me state absolutely and categorically that Tom Nevin was never at any stage a member of the republican movement. Had he been, you would have seen some sort of gesture at his funeral and, at the very least, a commemoration, with some if not all of the republican trappings. Catherine made all the running in that department. Tom never got involved. He didn't consort with any of the known republicans and he rarely spoke to them, except maybe to exchange niceties. In Tom's eyes everyone was the same, and as a result everybody was comfortable with him. The only differentiation he ever made between people was what drink they enjoyed.'

Gerry Heapes feels much the same. When I gave my evidence in court,' he says, 'the one thing I wanted to do was to let the Nevins know that we hadn't left Tom high and dry – that I had told people who went down to warn Catherine that she wasn't to touch Tom and any attempt to organise a hit on Tom would have repercussions for her and whoever she got to do it. This was all in my statement, but in court I never really got to say what I wanted to say. After I left the box, I sent a message to them through a guard to tell them I did all I could at the time and I was sorry for their loss – whatever use my saying that is to them – but I don't know if they got the message. One of them had come up and thanked me at the taking of the depositions and that made things a great deal easier for me. It was the first time a republican like myself has given evidence in a trial like that and I just want the Nevins to know that it was a worthy cause.'

Heapes went on to describe Tom Nevin's alleged criminal links as 'ridiculous – total rubbish, if you ask me – and the desecration of Tom's good name. Anyone with the slightest doubt about the type of man Tom Nevin was needs to get their head seen to. He was a gentleman, if ever there was one – a culchie, but a gentleman all the same. I have never met anyone apart from Catherine who had a bad word to say about him. Don't get me wrong, he wasn't all sweetness and light, but he just kept himself to himself and did his job. He never tried to pull a fast one on anyone, and the only thing that puzzles me about him is how in God's name he ever ended up with the likes of Catherine Nevin and why he didn't leave when the going was good. I'll never understand that.'

Willie McClean agrees. 'When she called me to the hospital and asked me to kill Tom,' McClean recalls, 'all I knew was I didn't want to be there or anywhere near her. In fact, I didn't want ever to see her again. She was just a liability. So I walked straight out of there and tried to forget about her. When I visited Jack White's three years later, she was so calm and friendly, I was beginning to think that it was all a bad dream – just a moment of madness on her part – until I heard that Tom had been killed. I felt really bad for Tom because I really liked the man, though I don't think the feeling was mutual, even if he was too well-bred to say so. It was a very strange situation, having an affair with a woman whose husband is still living under the same roof, but then a lot about Catherine Nevin was strange.

'As for Tom supposedly hanging about with crimi-nals, I can tell you now for a fact that Tom had no criminal tendencies – and I should know. There were people he knew who had done time, but then who doesn't know somebody who's done time. It doesn't mean that he ever got involved with them. Let me be blunt – and I will be accused of being sexist for saying this – but if Tom couldn't manage to keep control of his wife and was scared of her, he wouldn't have made much of a criminal, now would he? Although that doesn't say a lot for me, now does it?'

Why Tom Nevin chose to stay with his wife or why he feared the repercussions if he left, we will never know. It has been said that he was a proud man and, with one failed marriage behind him he would not contemplate another, but this is hardly justification for staying with a woman who has murderous intents.

We cannot be sure exactly when Catherine Nevin's reign of terror began, but we know that by 1994 Tom was a shivering wreck. Although she certainly threatened him with the IRA, among others, he must have realised, at least at this stage, that the IRA would not have sanctioned a hit like that. She may well have threatened to concoct a story about him and then have told him that, were he ever to leave her, she would tell the guards the story; they would believe her and his reputation would be in tatters. He had seen her do this to Gardaí Murphy and Whelan with devastating effect: she had effectively destroyed their careers. There was no reason for Tom to believe that she would not do it to him – or that she wasn't capable of carrying it out.

Yet he still loved her, despite the fact that she belittled him in front of Jack White's staff and had illicit affairs under his nose. He was protective of her, showered her with gifts and made sacrifices for her.

He valued their marriage even when it was a sham. There is no indication whatsoever that Catherine Nevin reciprocrated any of the affection he showed her. In fact, there is evidence, certainly from 1994 onwards, that she was physically abusing her husband. On several occasions, Tom sustained injuries that went unexplained. It seems that there were a few times when he stood up to her: these usually had to do with her suggestions that he sell her his half of Jack White's. But these instances were exceptions to the rule.

What happened behind closed doors in the Nevin household will continue to be the subject of speculation and rumour, but the end result was that an innocent and much-loved Galwayman came off worst in the end.